The Autism Cookbook
101 Gluten-Free and Allergen-Free Recipes

FREE FROM GLUTEN, EGG, MILK, RICE, SOY, PEANUT, TREE NUTS, FISH, AND SHELLFISH

Susan K. Delaine

Foreword by Dr. Peter Bauth
Introduction by Rebecca Peabody Estepp

Skyhorse Publishing

Skyhorse Publishing books may be purchased in bulk at special discounts for sales promotions, corporate gifts, fund-raising, or educational purposes. Special editions can also be created to specifications. For details, contact the Special Sales Department, Skyhorse Publishing, 307 West 36th Street, 11th Floor, New York, NY 10018 or info@skyhorsepublishing.com.

Skyhorse® and Skyhorse Publishing® are registered trademarks of Skyhorse Publishing, Inc.®, a Delaware corporation. Visit our website at www.skyhorsepublishing.com

10 9 8 7 6 5 4 3 2 1

Library of Congress Cataloging-in-Publication Data is available on file.
ISBN: 978-1-61608-653-4

Printed in China

This book is intended to be a resource for autism information and recipes. It is not intended to prevent, diagnose, treat or cure any condition or to provide medical advice. Consult a health or medical professional prior to making dietary changes.

Contents

Acknowledgments

Thank you Chris Delaine for your amazing mind, patience, strength, peace, will, order, wisdom, and understanding at all times. You are my pillar of strength. Justin and Ryan Delaine, thank you for the honor of being your mom. Parents, families, advocates for children with autism, thank you for writing this book. Children with autism, thank you for teaching the world about unconditional love.

Thank you Hester "Nena" Bell for your encouragement and friendship through the seasons. Thank you for the hard work and personal time you sacrificed to help me with this book.

Thank you Kareem Murphy and DeWayne Davis for your wisdom: unconditional love must prevail over tolerance. Your friendship divinely prepared me for the greatest challenge to love, years before its imminent arrival.

Thank you Delaine family, Kelley Family, Debra Nettles Woodard, Annabel Thomas, Ms. Rose, Jessica Schneider, Chris Snell (Fayette County Library), Dr. Peter Bauth, Connie Taylor (Meditating Mantis).

To all who have contributed to the greater good and who have helped spread awareness of this work, thank you!

Love, Susan

Author's Note

The title of this book expresses the purpose for which it is written. My intention is for you to experience joy and ease in your gluten-free, casein-free (GFCF) journey with your loved one. I have come to find that the key to great GFCF cooking lies in relaxing and enjoying the experience. Don't worry—everything else will flow.

Chances are, you have found this book because someone you love has autism, Attention Deficit Hyperactivity Disorder (ADHD), Attention Deficit Disorder (ADD), or a similar develop-mental challenge. You are interested in a biomedical approach to helping the person gain wellness in his or her body as a way to gain improvements in behavior, focus, attention, and physical comfort. You realize that removing offensive foods is one major part of the wellness approach for all people.

Our son was diagnosed with food allergies in 2001 (nine months old) and then diagnosed with autism in 2004 (age three). Within three weeks of changing his diet we began to see improvements in sleep, mood, and language. At that time, I wrote my first two gluten-free, casein-free, allergy-free cookbooks, *Balancing the Bowl 1 & 2*. Because of enormous demand for autism resources, my book has blossomed into *The Autism Cookbook*. We are convinced that a GFCF diet for children like our son is more of a health necessity than a choice.

How is this so? Many children with autism cannot digest gluten (a protein found in wheat, barley, rye, and contaminated in most oats) and casein (a protein found in cow's milk). This condition is called food intolerance or food sensitivity. Undigested food builds up in the digestive tract and becomes spoiled and toxic. This wreaks havoc on all body systems, including the brain. Thus, food affects behavior.

Visit the recommended websites listed on page 218 to further your understanding of cooking GFCF. If you choose to pursue it, you will find plenty of support from grocers, health professionals, educators, family members, and friends who will support you in your GFCF journey. While I have an enormous amount of confidence in your ability to make sound decisions for your child, I am legally obligated to advise you to consult with a medical professional prior to making a dietary change.

I hope you will enjoy these rich, international recipes, especially the Korean dishes, straight from my mother's kitchen. Most importantly, remember your true purpose for seeking a GFCF diet and worry less about making perfectly round pancakes. If your first batch is misshapen, then cut it up, dip it in maple syrup, and share it with someone you love!

Foreword

Health and wellness is all about addressing and correcting the cause; headaches do not result from a lack of aspirin. Indigestion is not a result from a lack of Pepcid. Depression is not a result of a lack of Wellbutrin, and autism is certainly not a condition resulting from a lack of medication. Autism has, as its origins, an imbalance of normal physiology. Addressing this aberrant physiology should be every parent's first impulse.

There are many ways to do this. However, with closer consideration, only a few approaches address the primary and the determining causes; the determining being chemical toxicity, physical traumatism, and emotional tendencies or stressors that lead to these aberrant functions; and the primary being the actual manifestation of these stressors, brain hemispheric deficiency, nutritional deficiency subluxation complex, and heavy metal toxicity.

For years now, clinicians and researchers have noticed positive changes in the physical and emotional health of children under chiropractic care, for example. Among the observed benefits are improvements in children with hyperactivity, autism, anxiety, low mental stamina, lack of concentration, asthma, and discipline problems. Improvement in grades and IQ have also been recorded.

Combine this now with the overwhelming body of evidence that shows direct connections between specific nutritional deficiencies and cognitive health and development issues, and one begins to see a positive paradigm shift emerging in healthcare and the standard treatment of these childhood conditions, such as autism—treatments that have, until recently, been largely ineffective.

In my practice and in the practice of many colleagues, care is given based on this different paradigm of health, and the results are nothing short of extraordinary. Give the information in this book a diligent try—you have nothing to lose and so very, very much to gain.

—Dr. Peter Bauth, D.C. LCP

Introduction

January 1, 2001 was "D-Day" for my family. No, we did not storm the beaches of Normandy, although at times I felt so challenged that it did seem like a war. In reality, our D-Day was different. The "D" stood for diet. It was on that day that my husband and I started our almost three-year-old son, Eric, on the gluten-free casein-free (GFCF) diet.

Eric was diagnosed with autism in November of 2000. We were given a grim prognosis by our pediatrician. I also remember having an overwhelming feeling that this trusted pediatrician knew nothing about autism and knew nothing about my son or my family.

Luckily, I found a great network of parents on the internet that were treating their children's symptoms through diet and supplements following the Defeat Autism Now (DAN) protocol. The GFCF diet was central to this treatment. Due to my son's bowel problems (alternating constipation and diarrhea) a diet made perfect sense to me.

My trusted group of veteran internet parents, who would later be the individuals to start Talk About Curing Autism (TACA), gave me guidance through the early days of GFCF. There was not much available to purchase at my local grocery store, so I took many trips to health food stores. I bought some items online and learned to cook like my Scottish grandmother—meat and potatoes for almost every dinner.

A short time later, Eric started to respond to the diet. The first improvement was the cessation of his night screaming. After that, Eric's mysterious fevers disappeared. And then a miracle happened—Eric started to behave much better than before the diet. I have to believe that it was simply because he felt better. Let's face it: all of us do better when we feel well.

My son is now thriving. He will be twelve in a few short weeks. I still classify him as a child with autism, although we have a few opinions from teachers and therapists that he doesn't meet the qualification for autism any longer, which shows fantastic progress. I know that the GFCF diet was the foundation for his improved state and could not have been attained unless we went through our diet "D-Day" so long ago.

—Rebecca Peabody Estepp, National Manager, TACA (Talk About Curing Autism)

The Autism Cookbook

Autism and Diet

Autism currently affects 1 in 110 children. Some signs of autism may appear during infancy. Other children develop normally and regress sharply between the ages of eighteen months to two years. The set of symptoms in autism will differ from person to person. Because symptoms range from very minor to very severe, autism is considered to be a "spectrum" disorder.

Research has shown that many autistic children have damaged intestinal tracts resulting from an overgrowth of bacteria. Some children are born with this condition. Other children are born with healthy digestive tracts and experience damage when exposed to environmental poisons, medications, processed and contaminated foods, and other toxins in our world. This damage can result in "food sensitivity" or "food intolerance," a condition in which the intestines cannot fully digest certain foods. Three common food sensitivity culprits are gluten (from wheat, barley, rye, and oat), casein (from cow's milk and goat's milk), and soy. Particles of foods left undigested in the intestine leak into the blood stream and have an adverse effect on the brain. This effect, similar to that of opiate drugs, can cause impairments in speech, motor skills, mood, focus, and learning and can worsen existing challenges. A diet free from gluten, casein, and soy (GFCFSF) can alleviate the discomfort a child is experiencing.

Like my son, Justin, many autistic children also have food allergies. A food allergy is a condition of the immune system in which the body "fights" against foods it believes to be harmful. This cookbook is exclusive of common food sensitivity culprits (gluten, casein, and soy) as well as some of the most common food allergens (wheat, rice, egg, milk, peanut, tree nuts, fish, and shellfish).

The gluten-free, casein-free, soy-free diet is the most common type of autism diet and is the focus of this book. However, there are other specific diets that can be used to meet the child's needs. It is helpful to work with a supportive healthcare professional who will provide testing, over time, to determine if your child's diet approach is working. Other diets include:

GFCF: Gluten Free, Casein Free

Specific Carbohydrate: A diet free from gluten, all starches (potato, corn, rice, all grains), and sugars. The diet allows specially cultured dairy products to be consumed. The goal of this diet is to stop the growth of microbes by eliminating foods that feed them.

Feingold Diet: Pinpoint and completely eliminate sensitivity culprits, allergens, chemicals, additives, and salicylates. These offending items are eliminated from both the diet and the environment (e.g., lotions, soaps, toothpaste, medicines, household products).

Elimination Diet: This diet is based on eliminating all major food allergens and sensitivity culprits, as well as eating free-range meats, specific fruits and vegetables, and rice-based milk and pastas. Its purpose is to identify and eliminate food culprits and reintroduce them gradually over a specified schedule. Elimination diets require close record-keeping of foods in correlation to behaviors.

Diet alone does not cure autism but removing offensive foods is one major portion of the healing process. To maximize the benefits of a GFCFSF diet, one should also take steps to heal the intestinal tract, support the immune system, and nurture the whole child through healing arts.

Why Raw?

Throughout this book you will find numerous raw recipes. Foods are considered to be "raw" if they have not been cooked above 118°F. A diet high in unprocessed, raw foods is a vital part of proper digestion and good health, and this is true for everyone. Raw foods contain their own enzymes to help us digest them with ease, without over-taxing the body. Because raw foods are so easy to digest, they are detoxifying, highly nutritious, and give a boost to the immune system. These are added benefits for everyone, especially for those with autism or allergies.

I do not recommend consuming raw eggs, meat, or fish. Rather, in this book you will find several raw recipes using fruits, vegetables, seeds, herbs, and cold-pressed oils. Raw foods can be eaten in their natural state or they can be prepared into recipes to satisfy your texture and flavor preferences. In my family's experience, adding one raw item to each meal every day (either a prepared raw dish or a side of raw fruits, vegetables, or seeds) had a great cumulative effect!

For those who have temperature preferences, raw foods can be heated up to 118°F and chilled while keeping their enzymes and nutrients intact. Our son, Justin, finds it easier to chew certain textures of foods that are at room temperature or warmed slightly. Use a food thermometer to heat raw foods safely.

Going Organic

Organic fruits, vegetables, and other crops have been grown without the use of artificial pesticides, fertilizers, or Genetically Modified Organisms (GMOs). Organic animals have been raised without the use of antibiotics or growth hormones and have been fed an organic crop diet. In most cases, organic animals being raised for food are uncaged and allowed to roam freely. Therefore, they are leaner, stronger, and naturally disease-free. Because organic foods contain minimal additives, they maintain a natural state and are much easier to digest than non-organic foods.

The U.S. Department of Agriculture (USDA) has established standards for allowing foods to be labeled as "USDA Organic." Individual organic farmers who wish to use the USDA Organic labels must meet these standards and undergo yearly inspections to assure compliance. There are three types of USDA Organic products:

100% Organic (the food label is allowed to display the "USDA Organic" symbol)

Organic (at least 95 percent of the ingredients are organic)

Made with Organic Ingredients (70 percent of the ingredients are organic; 30 percent contain no GMOs).

Replacements

USE...	INSTEAD OF...	FOR...
Quinoa Tapioca Millet Buckwheat Amaranth	Wheat Barley Rice Oat	Side dish Baking
Corn Quinoa	Wheat Rice	Whole grain baking Cereal baking/frying Pasta
Baking soda Baking powder (aluminum-free)	Egg	Leavening in baking
Potato flour Buckwheat flour Corn flour	Wheat flour Rice flour	Breading/frying and thickening
Potato Buckwheat Quinoa	Rice	Side dish
Applesauce Water	Milks (cow's, rice, and soy)	Moisture in baking
Safflower oil Corn oil Olive oil (cold-pressed oils are best)	Butter "Vegetable" oil (usually another name for soybean oil)	Frying and sautéing Moisture Dressings
Flax seed Sesame seed Pumpkin and Sunflower seed	Peanuts Tree nuts Soy nuts	"Nutty" flavoring Alternative to nut butters Alternative to nuts
Ginger, sesame, and garlic combined	Soy sauce	Flavor in Asian dishes
Honey Agave nectar Evaporated cane juice Xylitol Stevia	White granulated sugar	Sweetener

Guide to Reading Food Labels

Always check ingredient labels every time you buy a packaged product. Manufacturers will frequently change the recipe, the manufacturing process, or the vendors who supply ingredients. Sometimes an allergen may be introduced with each subsequent change. If you are unsure of the product's "safeness," contact the manufacturer to ask.

The Food Allergy Labeling Consumer Protection Act of 2006 requires food manufacturers to clearly indicate the presence of the top eight allergens on food labels: peanuts, tree nuts, milk, eggs, fish, shellfish, wheat, and soy.

Words Indicating Gluten

Barley
Caramel color
Flour
Hydrolyzed Vegetable Protein (HVP)
Malt
Modified food starch
Monosodium Glutamate (MSG)
Oat
Rye
Spelt

Stabilizers
Starch
Sweetener
Triticale
Wheat

Foods Containing Gluten

Barley pearls
Beers (barley)
Breads and breading
Cake

Cold cereals
Cookies
Custard
Crackers
Cream of wheat
Crusts

Muffins
Oatmeal
Oat flour
Pasta

Pretzels
Sausages
Soft tortillas
Soy sauce
Soups
Starchy foods listed as "wheat-free"

Deli meat
Distilled vinegar
Granola bars
Gravy
Hot dogs

Words Indicating Casein (Milk)

Caramel coloring
Cream
Dairy
Lactalbumin
Lactoglobulin
"Lactose-free"
Maltodextrin
Whey

Foods Containing Casein (Milk)

Butter
Cheeses
(Milk) Chocolate
Cow's milk
Custard
Deli meat
Goat's milk (its protein is similar to cow's milk)
Hot dogs

Ice cream
Imitation cheeses
"Non-dairy" creamer
Puddings
Salad dressings
Sauces
Sausages
Smoothies
Yogurt

Words Indicating Egg	Foods Containing Egg	Words Indicating Tree Nuts	Foods Containing Tree Nuts
Albumin	Baked goods (breads, cakes, cookies, crusts, etc.)	(Often cross-contaminated with peanut products and seeds)	Candy bars
Dairy			Cookies
Emulsifier	Egg substitute		
Globulin	Mayonnaise	Almonds	Flavored coffees
Livetin	Powdered eggs	Brazil nuts	Nut butters
Ovomucin	Quiche	Cashews	Salads
Ovomucoid		Chestnuts	Thai dishes
Vitelin		Hazelnuts	Trail mixes
		Macadamia nuts	

Words Indicating Soy	Foods Containing Soy
Caramel color	Chocolate candy
Emulsifier	Hot dogs
Protein	Salad dressings
Textured Vegetable Protein (TVP)	Smooth beverages
Vegetable protein	Soy milk
	Soy sauce
	Tofu
	Vegan dishes
	"Vegetable" oil
	Vegetarian dishes

Words Indicating Tree Nuts (continued):
Pecans
Pine nuts
Pistachios
Walnuts

Words Indicating Rice	Foods Containing Rice
Maltodextrin	Brown rice
Starch	Corn cakes (some brands)
	Rice cakes
	Rice cereal
	Rice milk
	Starchy foods listed as "gluten-free" or "wheat-free"
	Wild rice

Words Indicating Peanut	Foods Containing Peanut
Green peas (direct relative of peanut)	Nuts (high chance for cross-contamination during processing)
Peanut butter	
Peanut oil	
Peanuts	
	Trail mixes
	Roasted seeds (high chance for cross-contamination during processing)

Words Indicating Fish/Shellfish	Foods Containing Fish/Shellfish
Anchovy	Asian dishes, sauces
Caviar	Cajun dishes
Crab	Imitation crabmeat
Fish	Pizza topping
Lobster	Seafood salad
Mussels	Surf and turf menus
Sardine	
Scallops	
Seafood	
Shrimp	
Tuna	

Using This Book

Brand names and procedures recommended for these recipes:

Buckwheat flours:
Bouchard Family Farms "Acadian" Light Buckwheat Flour: Guaranteed to be free from gluten contamination. Go to www.ployes.com or call 1-800-239-3237 or (207) 834-3237 to order or for a list of retailers.

Birkett Mills Pocono Light/Dark Buckwheat Flour Mix: Best efforts made to avoid cross contamination from other products. Go to www.thebirkettmills.com or call 315-536-9296 to order or for retail information.

Dark Buckwheat Flour:
Arrowhead Mills Organic Buckwheat Flour, found in most grocery stores and health food stores.

Quinoa Flour:
Ancient Harvest (www.quinoa.net), found in most health food stores, grocers or order online.

Amaranth Flour, Potato Flour, Tapioca Flour, and Flaxseed Meal: Bob's Red Mill, found in health food stores, most grocers or order at www.bobsredmill.com.

Millet Flour:
Arrowhead Mills, found in health food stores and most grocers.

Cornmeals:
Hodgson Mill Yellow Cornmeal found in most grocery stores and Arrowhead Mills Organic Yellow Cornmeal, found in most health food stores and some grocers.

Pasta:
Ancient Harvest Quinoa-Corn Blend (www.quinoa.net), found in health food stores or most grocers.

Quinoa Seeds:
Ancient Harvest (www.quinoa.net) and NOW (www.nowfoods.com), both available in health food stores.

Buckwheat "Seeds" or Granules:
Wolff's Kasha (www.wolffskasha.com), available in most grocery and health food stores.

Quinoa Flakes:
Ancient Harvest (www.quinoa.net), see health food stores or most grocers.

GF Vanilla Extract:
McCormick, found in most grocery stores.

Aluminum-Free Baking Powders:
Rumford Aluminum-Free Baking Powder, found in most grocery stores (red packaging) and Everyday 365 found in Whole Foods.

Raw, Unfiltered Apple Cider Vinegar: Braggs and Spectrum, found in most health food stores and grocery stores.

Palm Oil Shortening: Spectrum, found in most health food stores and grocery stores.

Raw Seeds (pumpkin, sesame and sunflower): NOW (www.nowfoods.com), found in most health food stores.

GFCF Chocolate Chips: Enjoy Life, found in most grocery stores and health food stores.

Cocoa Powder: Hershey's (available in dark cocoa and regular cocoa), found in most grocery stores.

Turkey Kielbasa Sausage: Wellshire Farms (www.wellshirefarms.com), found at Whole Foods and some grocery stores.

Coconut Water: O.N.E. and VitaCoco, found in health food stores and some grocery stores.

Recipes requiring ground turkey were prepared using 93% lean turkey.

Steamed quinoa is used in lieu of rice in this book because of my son's rare allergy to rice. If desired and if tolerable, use steamed rice as a side dish in place of steamed quinoa.

Some flours are more readily available than others. For your convenience, most baked recipes offer one or more flour options.

All baked goods should be used, frozen, or discarded within 24 hours. Preservatives and additives are minimal (especially when using organic products), so shelf life is very short.

All stovetop and baked recipes were prepared using a conventional, electric stove and oven. Recipes prepared using a gas stove or oven will require less cooking time (10-15 mins less, on average).

Refrigerate leftovers from all cooked dishes after cooled. Leftovers can be refrigerated for up to 48 hours. Use, freeze, or discard leftovers after 48 hours.

Refrigerate leftovers from raw dishes. Keep for up to 48 hours after preparation. Discard leftovers after 48 hours.

"If you will allow even the slightest opening, if you can have just a bit of curiosity and hope about what might be possible, then I promise that miracles are just around the corner."

—Suzy Miller, *Awesomism*

Main Dishes

The Autism Cookbook

1

Apple Chicken Sausage

1 LB GROUND CHICKEN
1 MEDIUM APPLE (ANY VARIETY),
  PEELED AND FINELY CHOPPED
1 TABLESPOON GROUND SAGE
1 TEASPOON SALT
1 TABLESPOON MOLASSES
2 TEASPOONS GROUND BLACK
  PEPPER

1. Combine all ingredients in a bowl and mix until well blended. Cover tightly and refrigerate at least 3 hours (best results if marinated overnight).

2. Use hands to form small sausage patties. Heat a frying pan to medium and cook 3-4 patties until done on each side.

Hamburger Pie

½ LB GROUND BEEF OR TURKEY

1 SMALL ONION, CHOPPED

1 TEASPOON EACH OF SALT, BLACK
  PEPPER, AND GARLIC POWDER

½ TEASPOON CRUSHED THYME

½ CUP EACH OF FROZEN CORN AND
  SLICED CARROTS

¼ CUP TOMATO SAUCE

¼ CUP WATER

½ BATCH OF CORNBREAD BATTER
  (RECIPE FROM PAGE 117)

1. Preheat oven to 400°F.

2. Combine meat and onion in a large pan. Cook over medium heat until meat is browned. Drain the fat.

3. Add salt, pepper, garlic powder, thyme, and vegetables. Stir until blended and vegetables are thawed.

4. Stir in tomato sauce and water. Pour all ingredients into a 9-inch round pie pan. Pour cornbread batter over top of the meat. If needed, use a rubber spatula to spread the batter.

5. Bake for 25-30 mins until cornbread appears light brown and crusty.

Chicken and Dumplings

2 BONELESS, SKINLESS CHICKEN
   BREASTS
1 SMALL ONION, PEELED AND CUT
   INTO FOURTHS
1 STALK CELERY, CHOPPED
2 CUPS PEELED AND SLICED CARROTS
3 WHOLE BAY LEAVES
½ TEASPOON CRUSHED OR GROUND
   THYME
½ TEASPOON GROUND BLACK PEPPER
SALT TO TASTE (UP TO 1 TEASPOON)
5 CUPS WATER

DUMPLINGS
½ CUP LIGHT BUCKWHEAT FLOUR
2 TABLESPOONS TAPIOCA FLOUR
½ TEASPOON SALT
1 TABLESPOON PALM OIL
   SHORTENING
1 TABLESPOON WATER

1. In a 3 quart pot, combine chicken, onion, celery, carrots, bay leaves, thyme, black pepper, salt, and water. Stir to combine ingredients.

2. Bring to a boil and reduce temperature to low. Cover and simmer on low 40-50 mins or until chicken is very tender. Stir occasionally.

3. Meanwhile, prepare dumplings. Stir together flours and salt in a small bowl. Add shortening and water. Stir until a sticky dough forms. Set aside until chicken has finished cooking.

4. Open the lid and skim off bay leaves. Shred the chicken with a large metal spoon or fork.

5. While the broth is still simmering, scoop 1 tablespoon of dumpling dough and use floured hands (buckwheat) to flatten to ¼ inch thickness. Drop the dough into the pot and repeat until all of the dough is used. Remove from heat immediately—dumplings should cook for no more than 2 mins.

6. Stir and serve warm. Chicken and dumplings may be served with or without the broth.

Chicken Fingers

CORN OR SAFFLOWER OIL FOR FRYING
1   CUP CORNMEAL OR LIGHT
    BUCKWHEAT FLOUR
½   TEASPOON SALT
1   TEASPOON GROUND BLACK PEPPER
1   LARGE BONELESS, SKINLESS
    CHICKEN BREAST, CUT INTO 6-8
    SMALL SLICES

1. Preheat oil in a deep fryer.

2. Line a plate with two layers of paper towels. Set aside.

3. Combine cornmeal or flour, salt and black pepper in a medium bowl. Stir and set aside.

4. Wash chicken and cut into 6 to 8 slices.

5. Place chicken slices in the bowl with the corn meal or flour. Cover chicken thoroughly.

6. Deep-fry approximately 2 mins or until chicken appears light brown. Stir frequently to prevent chicken from sticking together.

7. Remove from oil. Place on the lined plate to drain excess oil.

8. Cool before serving.

Easy Chicken Quinoa Casserole

1 LARGE CHICKEN BREAST
1 CUP UNCOOKED QUINOA SEEDS
2 CUPS CHICKEN BROTH
2 TABLESPOONS OLIVE OIL
1 SMALL ONION, MINCED
1 CELERY STALK, CHOPPED
1 RED BELL PEPPER, SLICED INTO
  CIRCLES

1. Preheat oven to 400°F.

2. Slice chicken breast along the middle to make two thin cutlets. Place in a bowl and season as desired. If your chicken broth contains salt, you may want to omit salt from the seasoning. Set aside.

3. Pour quinoa seeds into a 9-inch baking dish. Add broth, oil, onion, and celery and stir until quinoa is submerged.

4. Top with chicken breasts and bell peppers.

5. Cover tightly and bake 30-40 mins until all broth is absorbed into the quinoa seeds.

Chicken Nuggets

RECIPE 1
(BREADING IS MIXED INTO THE NUGGETS)

CORN OR CANOLA OIL FOR FRYING
¼ CUP POTATO FLOUR
1   TEASPOON SALT
½ LB GROUND CHICKEN
¼ TEASPOON DRIED, CRUSHED THYME
     LEAVES
½ TEASPOON GROUND BLACK PEPPER
½ TEASPOON ONION POWDER
¼ TEASPOON GROUND THYME
     (OPTIONAL)

RECIPE 2
(BREADING COVERS THE NUGGETS)

CORN OR SAFFLOWER OIL FOR FRYING
½ POUND GROUND CHICKEN
½ TEASPOON SALT
½ TEASPOON GROUND BLACK PEPPER
½ TEASPOON ONION POWDER
¼ TEASPOON GROUND THYME
(OPTIONAL)
1 CUP LIGHT BUCKWHEAT FLOUR FOR
DUSTING

1. Preheat corn or safflower oil in a deep fryer.

2. Line a plate with two layers of paper towels.

3. For recipe 1, mix together all nugget ingredients in a small bowl. Create half-dollar sized nuggets with hands. Cook in deep fryer for approximately 60-90 seconds until nuggets appear light brown. Stir frequently. Remove and place on paper towels to drain oil. Cool before serving.

4. For recipe 2, place light buckwheat flour in a small bowl and set aside. Mix together all other nugget ingredients in a small bowl. Create half-dollar sized nuggets with hands and dip each nugget in the buckwheat flour to coat. Shake off excess flour. Cook in deep fryer for approximately 60-90 seconds until nuggets appear light brown. Stir frequently. Remove and place on paper towels to drain oil. Cool before serving.

Serve with Honey Mustard Dipping Sauce on page 211.

Chicken-Sausage Ratatouille

¼ CUP OLIVE OIL
2 BONELESS, SKINLESS CHICKEN BREASTS, CUBED
2 CUPS SMOKED SAUSAGE OR KIELBASA, SLICED
4 GARLIC CLOVES, MINCED
1 CUP ZUCCHINI SQUASH, CUBED
1 CUP EGGPLANT, PEELED AND CUBED
1 CUP RED BELL PEPPER, CHOPPED
1 CUP WATER
2 CUPS TOMATO, CUBED
1 TABLESPOON DRIED, CRUSHED OREGANO
5 FRESH BASIL LEAVES, CHOPPED

1. In a medium saucepan, combine oil and meat. Cook over medium temperature until chicken is slightly brown, stirring constantly.

2. Stir in garlic, zucchini, eggplant, and bell pepper. Cook until zucchini is slightly soft.

3. Stir in water, tomatoes, oregano, and basil. The mixture should be very thick.

4. Cover tightly and let simmer on low heat for 25-30 mins. Stir occasionally to prevent sticking to the bottom.

5. Cool slightly and serve.

Chunky Red Bean Chili

½ LB GROUND TURKEY OR GROUND
   CHUCK BEEF
½ CUP EXTRA VIRGIN OLIVE OIL
1 SMALL GREEN PEPPER, CHOPPED
½ CUP ONION, CHOPPED
2 GARLIC CLOVES, MINCED
2 TABLESPOONS GROUND CUMIN
½ TEASPOON BLACK PEPPER
½ TEASPOON SALT
1 CAN (14–16 OUNCES) RED BEANS,
   DRAINED (DO NOT RINSE)
2 CUPS TOMATO SAUCE
½ CUP FRESH CILANTRO LEAVES,
   CHOPPED

1. In a medium pot, brown the meat. Drain any excess fat.

2. Add olive oil, green pepper, onion, garlic, cumin, black pepper, and salt. Simmer over low heat until vegetables are soft. Stir occasionally.

3. Add drained beans and tomato sauce. Stir until blended.

4. Simmer over very low heat for approximately 1 hour, stirring occasionally.

5. Add cilantro. Stir and continue to simmer over very low heat for an additional 30 mins. Chili will thicken.

Chunky Vegetable Chili (Raw)

CHILI

1	PORTOBELLO MUSHROOM, CUBED
1	MEDIUM ZUCCHINI, CUBED
1	LARGE TOMATO, CUBED
1	SMALL ONION, CHOPPED
1	TEASPOON SALT
2	TABLESPOONS CUMIN POWDER
3	TABLESPOONS COLD-PRESSED OLIVE OIL

JUICE OF 1 LARGE LEMON

SAUCE

2	LARGE TOMATOES, CUBED
4	SUNDRIED TOMATOES
1	GARLIC CLOVE
1	CUP FRESH CILANTRO LEAVES
2	TABLESPOONS GROUND CUMIN
½	TEASPOON SALT
2	TABLESPOONS OLIVE OIL
1	CUP WATER

1. Combine chili ingredients in a large bowl. Stir until well blended.

2. Cover tightly and let marinate 30 mins at room temperature.

3. Prepare sauce: Combine all sauce ingredients in a blender. Blend until smooth.

4. Add sauce to chili ingredients and stir until well blended.

5. Cover tightly and let marinate at room temperature for 1 hour.

6. If desired, warm slightly to no more than 118°F.

Cuban Black Beans

¼ CUP EXTRA VIRGIN OLIVE OIL
½ GREEN PEPPER, CHOPPED
1 SMALL ONION, CHOPPED
3 GARLIC CLOVES, CHOPPED
½ TEASPOON GROUND CUMIN
½ TEASPOON BLACK PEPPER
1 CAN (14–16 OUNCES) UNSEASONED
   BLACK BEANS—DO NOT DRAIN OR
   RINSE
½ LB COOKED MEAT, SUCH AS SMOKED
   TURKEY OR ROASTED PORK, IF
   DESIRED

1. Combine olive oil, green pepper, onion, garlic, cumin, and black pepper in a small saucepan. Stir while simmering on low until vegetables are soft.

2. Add black beans (with liquid). Stir until well blended.

3. Simmer over very low heat; add cooked meat for flavor if desired. Cook for 45 mins. Stir occasionally.

Serve warm over a baked potato or over Steamed Quinoa or Buckwheat with Veggies on page 98.

Curried Chicken or Beef

5 BONELESS, SKINLESS CHICKEN THIGHS OR 1 POUND SIRLOIN BEEF CUBES
2 TABLESPOONS EXTRA-VIRGIN OLIVE OIL
1 MEDIUM ONION, PEELED AND SLICED
1 MEDIUM GREEN BELL PEPPER, SLICED
1½ CUPS WATER
1 RUSSET POTATO, PEELED AND CUBED
4 GARLIC CLOVES, MINCED
¼ CUP FRESH CILANTRO, CHOPPED

SEASONING MIX
1 TABLESPOON EACH GROUND CUMIN, CORIANDER, TURMERIC, AND GINGER
½ TEASPOON GROUND CINNAMON (OPTIONAL)
1 TABLESPOON DRIED OR CRUSHED THYME LEAVES
½ TEASPOON SALT
1 TEASPOON GROUND BLACK PEPPER

1. Combine seasoning mix ingredients in a small bowl and stir to blend. Set aside.

2. Wash meat thoroughly and drain excess water. Trim and discard excess fat.

3. In a large saucepan, heat olive oil and brown the meat lightly on all sides. Stir in onion and green bell pepper. Cook for 1 minute.

4. Stir in water, potatoes and seasoning mix. Stir until blended. Bring to a simmer.

5. Reduce heat to low and cook 25 to 30 mins or until meat is soft.

6. Open the lid and toss in garlic and cilantro. Do not stir. Cover and simmer an additional 10 mins.

Makes 5 to 6 servings. Serve over steamed quinoa.

Grilled Chicken Skewers

5   BONELESS, SKINLESS CHICKEN
    THIGHS
¼   CUP ROASTED SESAME OIL
2   TABLESPOONS EVAPORATED CANE
    JUICE OR AGAVE NECTAR
1   TEASPOON SALT
2   TABLESPOONS GROUND GINGER
    POWDER
2   GARLIC CLOVES, MINCED

1. Wash and trim excess fat from chicken thighs.

2. Cut chicken into 2-inch slices.

3. Combine chicken slices and all ingredients in a medium bowl. Stir until well blended.

4. Cover and refrigerate. Let marinate at least 20 mins.

5. Place chicken slices on individual skewers.

6. Place skewers on grill over medium heat. Cook thoroughly on each side until done.

Dip in warm Sesame or Pumpkin "Butter" on page 203 or serve with Steamed Quinoa or Buckwheat with Veggies on page 98.

Maple-Glazed Chicken Legs

6   MEDIUM CHICKEN LEGS
1   CUP 100% MAPLE SYRUP
½   CUP RAW APPLE CIDER VINEGAR
1   TEASPOON OLIVE OIL
½   TEASPOON SALT
1   TEASPOON BLACK PEPPER
1   TEASPOON CURRY SEASONING
    (OPTIONAL)

1. In a small mixing bowl, combine all ingredients except for chicken. Stir with a whisk until blended.

2. In a large freezer bag, combine glaze ingredients and chicken legs. Seal the bag and use your hands to gently blend the maple seasoning into the chicken from the outside of the bag.

3. Refrigerate for 1 hour.

4. Preheat oven to 400°F.

5. Place chicken in a glass baking dish and cover chicken lightly with extra marinade. Do not allow for too much marinade to cover the bottom of the pan. Discard remaining marinade.

6. Bake for 45-60 mins.

Meatballs with Sweet Glaze

GLAZE
1   RECIPE BARBECUE SAUCE FROM
    PAGE 201
½   CUP AGAVE NECTAR

MEATBALLS
1   POUND GROUND BEEF OR TURKEY
½   CUP BREADCRUMBS FROM PAGE 122
    OR ½ CUP FLAXSEED MEAL
1   TEASPOON EACH GARLIC POWDER
    AND ONION POWDER
½   TEASPOON SALT
1   TEASPOON GROUND BLACK PEPPER
2   TABLESPOONS EXTRA-VIRGIN OLIVE
    OIL FOR BROWNING

1. Prepare glaze. In a medium bowl, combine barbecue sauce and agave nectar. Stir until blended, then set aside.
2. Prepare meatballs. In another medium bowl, combine all meatball ingredients. Stir until well blended and smooth. Form 2-inch meatballs with hands.
3. In a large frying pan, heat olive oil to medium heat. Cook meatballs on each side until light brown.
4. Pour glaze over meatballs. Bring to a simmer and reduce heat to low.
5. Cover and cook for 20 mins, stirring occasionally.

Makes 3 to 4 servings.

Meatloaf

1½ LBS LEAN GROUND BEEF OR
   TURKEY
1   SMALL ONION, FINELY CHOPPED
½   SMALL GREEN PEPPER, FINELY
   CHOPPED
½   CUP BREADCRUMBS ON PAGE 122
   OR ½ CUP FLAXSEED MEAL
4   TABLESPOONS EXTRA VIRGIN OLIVE
   OIL
1½ CUPS TOMATO SAUCE
1   TABLESPOON DRIED, CRUSHED
   OREGANO LEAVES
2   TABLESPOONS GARLIC POWDER
1   TEASPOON BLACK PEPPER
½   TEASPOON SALT (OPTIONAL)

TOPPINGS
½   CUP TOMATO SAUCE OR KETCHUP
1   TEASPOON DRIED, CRUSHED
   OREGANO LEAVES

OPTIONAL ADD-INS
1   CUP CHOPPED SPINACH
1   TEASPOON GROUND TUMERIC AND/
   OR CUMIN

1. Preheat oven to 400°F.

2. Combine all meatloaf ingredients in a large mixing bowl. Mix well with a large fork until the mixture is smooth.

3. Spread meat evenly into a 9 x 5-inch loaf pan.

4. Smooth tomato sauce or ketchup over the top. Sprinkle lightly with oregano.

5. Bake on middle rack of oven until sides of meatloaf are slightly brown and crusty (approximately 45 mins).

6. Remove from pan to a serving dish.

Serve with Fluffy Mashed Potatoes on page 70.

Orange Chicken Wings

SAFFLOWER OR CORN OIL FOR DEEP
   FRYING
10 CHICKEN WING PIECES
¼ CUP EVAPORATED CANE JUICE
½ TEASPOON SALT
2 TABLESPOONS MINCED GINGER (OR
   1 TABLESPOON GINGER POWDER)
2 GARLIC CLOVES, MINCED (OR 1
   TABLESPOON GARLIC POWDER)
¼ CUP FRESH ORANGE PEEL, MINCED

1. Wash and pat dry the chicken wing pieces. Place in a medium bowl.

2. Preheat oil in a deep fryer. Line a plate with paper towels. Set aside.

3. Add all ingredients to chicken and mix until chicken is covered with seasonings.

4. Carefully place 4 to 6 chicken pieces into hot oil. Use more or less pieces, depending on your fryer's size.

5. Stir frequently and cook until wings are golden brown.

6. Remove from fryer and place on the lined plate to drain oil.

7. Cook remaining chicken pieces until wings are golden brown.

8. Cool before serving.

Thin Pizza Crust

CRUST

FLOUR OPTIONS

1   CUP LIGHT OR DARK BUCKWHEAT
    FLOUR

OR

1   CUP QUINOA FLOUR

2   TABLESPOONS TAPIOCA FLOUR
2   TABLESPOONS FLAXSEED MEAL
    (RECOMMENDED)
½   TEASPOON SALT
1   TABLESPOONS BAKING POWDER
    (ALUMINUM-FREE)
1   TEASPOON DRIED, CRUSHED
    OREGANO LEAVES (RECOMMENDED)
½   TEASPOON GARLIC POWDER
¼   CUP EXTRA-VIRGIN OLIVE OIL
½ TO ¾ CUP WATER (UP TO 1 CUP
WATER IF USING DARK BUCKWHEAT
    FLOUR)
LIGHT OR DARK BUCKWHEAT FLOUR OR
    QUINOA FLOUR FOR DUSTING

SUGGESTED TOPPINGS

TOMATO SAUCE
FRESH OR DRIED BASIL
FRESH OR DRIED GARLIC POWDER
NITRATE FREE PEPPERONI
COOKED, CHOPPED ITALIAN SAUSAGE
SLICED, GRILLED CHICKEN

CHOPPED GREEN BELL PEPPER
THINLY-SLICED ROMA TOMATOES
FRESH SPINACH, CHOPPED

1. Preheat oven to 400°F.

2. Prepare crust. In a medium bowl, combine dry
   ingredients and stir until blended.

3. Add oil and water and stir with a rubber spatula. If
   needed, slowly add no more than ¼ cup more water
   until dough sticks together. The dough should appear
   moist and fluffy. Use the spatula to gather the dough
   into a mound in the center of the bowl.

4. Use the spatula to guide the dough onto the center of
   a cookie sheet or pizza pan (13 inches).

5. Lightly dust the top of the dough with light or dark
   buckwheat flour and press down with fingers to
   create a flat, round crust. If too sticky, continue to
   lightly dust the surface while spreading the dough

6. Pour approximately ½ cup of tomato sauce on the
   center of the dough. Use a spoon to spread the sauce.
   Add desired toppings.

7. Bake 20 mins, or until crust is firm to the touch.

Makes 2 to 3 servings

Pumpkin Seed & Apple Stuffed Chicken

1 TABLESPOON CORN OR SAFFLOWER OIL FOR SAUTÉING

½ TEASPOON EACH OF SALT AND GROUND BLACK PEPPER

¼ CUP ONION, FINELY CHOPPED

½ CUP ROASTED PUMPKIN SEEDS, FINELY CHOPPED IN FOOD PROCESSOR

1 TABLESPOON FLAXSEED MEAL

½ CUP CORNMEAL

¼ CUP APPLE, PEELED AND FINELY CHOPPED (ANY VARIETY)

½ TEASPOON EACH OF GROUND CINNAMON, CARDAMOM, AND NUTMEG

½ CUP WATER

2 LARGE BONELESS, SKINLESS CHICKEN BREASTS, SLICED HORIZONTALLY TO SPREAD OPEN.

1. Preheat oven to 400°F.

2. Pour oil, salt, pepper, and onion into a small skillet and cook over low heat until vegetables are soft. In a medium mixing bowl, combine cooked onion and all other ingredients except chicken. Stir until well blended. The stuffing should be very thick.

3. Cut open the chicken breasts and lay flat. Scoop 2-3 tablespoons of stuffing mix and spread onto one side of the chicken. Fold the chicken to close.

4. Place stuffed chicken on a baking dish two inches apart. Brush lightly with oil. Bake uncovered for 45 mins. Cool slightly. Slice and serve.

Quick Stew

5 BONELESS, SKINLESS CHICKEN
THIGHS OR 1 LB SIRLOIN BEEF
CUBES
¼ CUP EXTRA VIRGIN OLIVE OIL
3 CUPS FRESH TOMATO, CUBED
1 MEDIUM ONION, SLICED
2 TABLESPOONS EACH OF DRIED,
CRUSHED BASIL, OREGANO, AND
THYME LEAVES
2 CUPS WATER
½ CUP POTATO, PEELED AND CUBED
4 GARLIC CLOVES, MINCED
SALT AND PEPPER TO TASTE

1. Use a large saucepan to heat olive oil over medium heat. Add chicken or beef and brown lightly on all sides.

2. Add tomatoes, onion, basil, oregano, and thyme.

3. Set temperature to low. Add water and potato, and cover lightly.

4. Simmer 30 mins for chicken and 60 mins for beef.

5. Lift lid and sprinkle garlic over top of meat. Do not stir.

6. Cover tightly again. Simmer on low for an additional 15 mins. Add salt and pepper to taste.

Serve over steamed quinoa or with Fluffy Mashed Potatoes on page 70.

Seed-Crusted Chicken Breast

2 TABLESPOONS OLIVE OIL
½ TEASPOON SALT
2 BONELESS, SKINLESS CHICKEN
BREASTS

CRUSTING

½ CUP PUMPKIN SEEDS (LIGHTLY
ROASTED WITHOUT OIL)
1 TABLESPOON FLAXSEED MEAL
½ TEASPOON GROUND CUMIN
½ TEASPOON GROUND CORIANDER
1 TEASPOON BLACK PEPPER

1. Season chicken breasts in oil and salt. Set aside.

2. Preheat oven to 400°F. Combine all crusting ingredients in a blender. Blend on high speed until ingredients are flaky. Pour into a medium bowl. Dip chicken into crusting, covering each side completely.

3. Place chicken on a lightly greased baking dish and bake uncovered for 45 mins or until chicken appears light brown.

Sesame-Ginger Chicken

5 BONELESS, SKINLESS CHICKEN THIGHS
½ CUP ROASTED SESAME OIL
3 TABLESPOONS FRESH GINGER, PEELED AND FINELY CHOPPED
UP TO 1 TEASPOON SALT
1 TEASPOON BLACK PEPPER
1 CUP WATER
5 GARLIC CLOVES, MINCED
½ GREEN PEPPER, CHOPPED
3 WHOLE SCALLIONS, SLICED
¼ CUP ROASTED SESAME SEEDS

1. Wash chicken thoroughly and drain excess water.

2. Remove excess fat with a knife and discard.

3. Combine meat, sesame oil, ginger, salt, and black pepper in a large bowl. Mix thoroughly

4. Brown the chicken on each side in a hot wok over medium heat (do not use additional oil).

5. Reduce temperature to medium-low. Add water and cover tighly. Simmer 30 mins or until chicken is tender.

6. Scatter garlic, green pepper, scallions, and sesame seeds over top of chicken. Do not stir.

7. Cover tightly again and simmer on low for an additional 15 mins.

Serve with a baked potato or with Asian Noodles on page 59. Also great with Steamed Quinoa or Buckwheat with Veggies on page 98.

Enchiladas

SAUCE
6 CUPS TOMATO SAUCE
2 TABLESPOONS GROUND CUMIN
1 TABLESPOON GARLIC POWDER
1 TEASPOON GROUND BLACK PEPPER
1 TEASPOON SALT

FILLING
1 LB GROUND BEEF OR TURKEY
OR
4 BONELESS SKINLESS CHICKEN
    CUTLETS
1 TABLESPOON EXTRA-VIRGIN OLIVE
    OIL
8 SOFT CORN TORTILLAS

1. Preheat oven to 400°F.

2. Prepare sauce. In a medium bowl. Combine sauce ingredients. Stir with a whisk and set aside.

3. Prepare filling. If using ground meat, cook the meat in a large frying pan until brown. Drain the fat. Stir in 2 cups of sauce and set aside. If using chicken, heat olive oil in a large frying pan. Cook the chicken on each side until well done. Remove from heat. Transfer chicken to a cutting board and cut into thin slices. Return chicken to pan and stir in 2 cups of sauce. Set aside.

4. Place tortillas on a microwave-safe dish and heat in microwave for 20 seconds to soften. Cool slightly. Hold 1 tortilla in the palm of your hand and spoon meat onto the center of the tortilla.

5. Fold the tortilla on each side to close. Place face down on a glass baking dish. Repeat until all tortillas have been used.

6. Pour remaining sauce over the enchiladas. Cover tightly and bake 25 mins.

7. Serve the enchiladas using a metal spatula to scoop.

Makes 8 enchiladas.

Sloppy Joe

1 LB GROUND BEEF OR TURKEY
1 SMALL GREEN BELL PEPPER, CHOPPED
1 SMALL ONION, PEELED AND CHOPPED
1 BARBEQUE SAUCE RECIPE FROM PAGE 201

1. Cook the ground meat in a large frying pan over medium heat until brown. Drain the fat.

2. Add green pepper and onion, and cook until soft. Stir frequently.

3. Stir in barbecue sauce and bring to a simmer.

4. Reduce temperature to low, cover and simmer for 10 mins, stirring halfway through.

Makes 5 to 6 servings. Serve with salad greens and a warm Cornbread Muffin on page 117 or serve over steamed quinoa.

Smothered Chicken

1   TABLESPOON OLIVE OIL
4   BONELESS, SKINLESS CHICKEN
     BREASTS
½   RED ONION, SLICED
1   RED BELL PEPPER, SLICED
½   TEASPOON SALT
½   TEASPOON GROUND BLACK PEPPER
½   TEASPOON GARLIC POWDER

GRAVY
3   CUPS CHICKEN BROTH
¼   CUP POTATO FLOUR
¼   TEASPOON SALT

1. Heat olive oil on low in a large skillet. Cook chicken until brown on each side. Add onions, bell peppers, salt, black pepper, and garlic powder. Cook until the onions are slightly brown. Cover and let simmer on the lowest setting.

2. Prepare gravy: Combine potato flour and broth in a large cup. Whisk until the flour is dissloved.

3. Pour potato flour mixture over chicken and bring to a simmer.

4. Reduce heat to low. Simmer for 20-30 mins or until chicken is tender. Stir frequently.

Stuffed Peppers

4 MEDIUM BELL PEPPERS, HOLLOWED
(ANY COLOR)
½ LB GROUND BEEF OR TURKEY
2 CUPS TOMATO SAUCE
4 GARLIC CLOVES, MINCED
1 SMALL ONION, FINELY CHOPPED
1 TEASPOON SALT
2 TEASPOONS CRUSHED OREGANO
LEAVES
½ CUP UNCOOKED BUCKWHEAT OR
QUINOA SEEDS

1. Preheat oven to 350°F.

2. Brown the meat in a medium saucepan. Drain fat. Add tomato sauce, garlic, onion, and seasonings. Simmer on low for 5 mins. Pour ingredients into a large mixing bowl and add buckwheat or quinoa seeds. Stir until well blended. Spoon the mixture into peppers until full.

3. Place peppers upright on a baking sheet and bake for 30 mins or until the edges of the peppers are lightly browned. Cool slightly before serving.

Thai Noodles with Sesame Butter Sauce

12 OUNCES OF UNCOOKED SPAGHETTI OR LINGUINE PASTA (CORN OR QUINOA VARIETIES)

2 TABLESPOONS OLIVE OIL

1 CUP SESAME BUTTER FROM PAGE 203

2 CUPS COCONUT WATER

1 TABLESPOON CURRY POWDER

1 TABLESPOON CUMIN POWDER

CRUSHED RED PEPPER TO TASTE (OPTIONAL)

1. Cook the pasta according to package directions. After draining, pour into a bowl. Add olive oil and stir. Set aside.

2. Prepare sesame butter recipe. Add coconut water, curry powder, and cumin powder. Stir until mixed.

3. Pour up to 1 cup of sesame butter mixture over pasta and stir until blended. Add crushed red pepper to taste (optional).

4. Serve warm with slices of grilled chicken if desired.

5. Refrigerate leftover sesame butter.

Thai Basil Chicken

1 TABLESPOON EXTRA-VIRGIN OLIVE
  OIL
5 GARLIC CLOVES, CHOPPED
3 SCALLIONS, CHOPPED
1 GREEN BELL PEPPER, SLICED
¼ TEASPOON SALT
3 BONELESS, SKINLESS CHICKEN
  BREASTS CUT INTO STRIPS
1 CUP FRESH BASIL LEAVES,
  CHOPPED
JUICE OF 1 LIME (OPTIONAL)

1. Heat oil to medium setting in a large pan. Add garlic, scallions, green pepper, basil leaves, and salt. Cook and stir until vegetables are soft.

2. Add chicken and stir frequently until chicken is well done (approximately 5 mins).

3. Remove from heat. Squeeze lime juice over top and stir.

Makes 4 to 5 servings. Serve over steamed quinoa.

Turkey Vegetable Toss

1 LB GROUND TURKEY (OR BEEF IF PREFERRED)
½ TEASPOON SALT
1 TEASPOON GROUND BLACK PEPPER
1 TEASPOON GROUND CUMIN
3 GARLIC CLOVES, MINCED
1 SMALL ONION, CHOPPED
1 SMALL GREEN BELL PEPPER, SLICED
1 CUP CORN KERNELS
1 CARROT, PEELED AND SLICED INTO CIRCLES (OR 1 CUP FROZEN, SLICED CARROT)
¼ CUP TOMATO SAUCE

1. In a large skillet, brown the meat. Drain excess fat.

2. Return to medium heat. Add salt, black pepper, cumin, garlic, onion, and green pepper. Stir and cook until vegetables are soft.

3. Add corn, carrot, and tomato sauce. Stir to blend.

4. Cover tightly and cook 10-15 mins or until the carrots are slightly soft.

Makes 4 to 5 servings. Serve over steamed quinoa.

Kabobs with Raw Red Curry Sauce

KABOBS

2 GRILLED BONELESS, SKINLESS
   CHICKEN BREASTS, CUBED, OR BEEF
   CUBES
1 GREEN AND 1 RED BELL PEPPER,
   CUBED AND GRILLED
1 ONION, CUBED AND GRILLED

SAUCE

2 CUPS O.N.E. COCONUT WATER
1 SMALL RED BELL PEPPER, SLICED
3 GARLIC CLOVES
2 TABLESPOONS COLD-PRESSED
   OLIVE OIL
2 TABLESPOONS CURRY POWDER
½ TEASPOON SALT

1. Alternate grilled meat, peppers, and onions on kabob sticks. Place the kabobs on serving plates and set aside.

2. Combine sauce ingredients in a blender and blend on high speed until smooth. For a thinner sauce, add coconut wate by the ¼ cup until desired consistency is reached.

3. Scoop sauce with a ladle and pour over kabobs.

Soups, Sides, and Salads

Artichoke Bean Dip with Raw Spinach

1   14–16 OUNCE CAN OF WHITE BEANS, DRAINED AND RINSED
¼   CUP EXTRA VIRGIN OLIVE OIL
6   LARGE GARLIC CLOVES, SLICED
UP TO 2 CUPS CHICKEN BROTH OR WATER
3   OUNCES BABY SPINACH LEAVES (APPROXIMATELY TWO HANDFULS)
1   3 OUNCE JAR OF MARINATED ARTICHOKE HEARTS, DRAINED
SALT TO TASTE

1. Combine beans, olive oil, sliced garlic, and 1 cup of broth (or water) in a blender.

2. Blend until beans are smooth and creamy. Add broth or water ¼ cup at a time if the mixture is too dry.

3. Add spinach and artichoke hearts. Pulse several times until the spinach and artichoke are coarsely chopped and mixed into the dip.

4, Heat slightly on stovetop if desired and add salt to taste.

Use this as a dip for tortilla chips.

Asian Noodles

1   LB GLUTEN–FREE SPAGHETTI

DRESSING
1½ CUP DARK SESAME OIL
1   TABLESPOON EVAPORATED CANE
    JUICE OR AGAVE NECTAR
½   TEASPOON SALT
1   TEASPOON BALSAMIC VINEGAR OR
    APPLE CIDER VINEGAR
1   GARLIC CLOVE, MINCED
1   SCALLION, SLICED
½   CUP ROASTED SESAME SEEDS
2   TEASPOONS GINGER POWDER

1. Boil spaghetti until tender. Do not over cook. Drain.

2. Rinse in cold water. Drain all excess water. Place spaghetti in a large bowl and set aside.

3. Combine all other ingredients and stir with a whisk until blended. Pour over spaghetti and toss.

Note: For a more authentic recipe, you may use Korean noodles made from sweet potato starch, known as "glass noodles." This can be found in Asian marketplaces.

Authentic Mango Salsa (Raw)

4   LARGE, RIPE TOMATOES, CUBED
1   LARGE, RIPE MANGO, PEELED AND
    CUBED
4   GARLIC CLOVES, MINCED
1   MEDIUM RED ONION, CHOPPED
2   WHOLE SCALLIONS, CHOPPED
2   CUPS FRESH CILANTRO LEAVES,
    CHOPPED
UP TO ½   TEASPOON SEA SALT
1   TEASPOON GROUND CUMIN
1   TEASPOON GROUND CORIANDER
JUICE OF 1 LARGE LEMON

1. Combine all ingredients, except lemon juice, in a
   large bowl.

2. Stir gently until ingredients are well distributed.

3. Squeeze lemon over the top.

4. Chill and serve with tortilla chips.

For a smoother texture, pulse 4-5 times in a food processor.

Broccoli Salad (Raw)

1   LB BROCCOLI CROWNS
½   CUP CORN OR SAFFLOWER OIL
4   TABLESPOONS APPLE CIDER
    VINEGAR
UP TO ½   TEASPOON SALT
3   TABLESPOONS EVAPORATED CANE
    JUICE OR RAW AGAVE NECTAR
1   TABLESPOON FRESH GINGER,
    PEELED AND FINELY CHOPPED,
OR 1 TEASPOON GROUND GINGER
    POWDER
1   CUP DRIED CRANBERRIES
¼   CUP RAW SESAME SEEDS OR RAW
    PUMPKIN SEEDS

1. Wash broccoli crowns thoroughly. Drain and set aside.

2. Combine oil, vinegar, salt, sweetener, and ginger in a large bowl. Blend thoroughly with a large whisk.

3. Pour broccoli into the bowl with the oil and vinegar mixture. Stir with a large spoon.

4. Add cranberries and seeds. Stir until blended.

5. Chill and serve.

Add cooked, chopped bacon if desired.

Chicken Salad

1 TABLESPOON OLIVE OIL
2 LARGE BONELESS, SKINLESS
  CHICKEN BREASTS
2 TABLESPOONS CORN OR
  SAFFLOWER OIL
¼ CUP APPLE CIDER VINEGAR
½ CUP GREEN PEPPER, FINELY
  CHOPPED
½ CUP CELERY, FINELY CHOPPED
3 TABLESPOONS ONIONS, FINELY
  CHOPPED
1 TABLESPOON SWEET RELISH
SALT AND PEPPER TO TASTE

1. Heat olive oil in a frying pan over medium heat. Cook chicken on both sides until well done.

2. Finely shred chicken in a blender by pulsing several times.

3. Place chicken in a bowl and add oil, vinegar, green pepper, celery, onion, and relish.

4. Stir with a fork until blended.

5. Add salt and pepper to taste and chill.

Place chicken salad over a bed of lettuce and serve with corn chips.

Cool Beans

2 CUPS BLACK BEANS, COOKED AND RINSED
1 CUP CILANTRO, CHOPPED
1 SCALLION, FINELY CHOPPED
1 SMALL ROMA TOMATO, CHOPPED
½ CUP CORN KERNELS
½ TEASPOON GROUND CUMIN
JUICE OF 1 SMALL LIME

1. Combine all ingredients in a medium bowl.

2. Toss gently.

3. Chill and serve with tortilla chips

Cornbread Stuffing

1 CORNBREAD MUFFIN RECIPE FROM PAGE 117
¼ CUP CELERY, CHOPPED
¼ CUP GREEN PEPPER, CHOPPED
¼ CUP ONION, CHOPPED
1 GARLIC CLOVE, CHOPPED
2 TABLESPOONS EXTRA VIRGIN OLIVE OIL
UP TO 32 OUNCES CHICKEN OR TURKEY BROTH
SALT AND BLACK PEPPER TO TASTE

1. Bake Cornbread Muffin recipe in a 8 or 9–inch square pan. Cool completely.

2. Preheat oven to 400°F.

3. Use a fork to crumble the cornbread inside the pan. Set aside.

4. Combine celery, green pepper, onion, garlic, and olive oil in a small saucepan. Simmer over low heat and stir until brown.

5. Add vegetables on top of cornbread mixture.

6. Add broth until cornbread is submerged. Stir gently.

7. Add salt and pepper to taste.

8. Bake uncovered on the middle rack of the oven until top and sides become crusty and stuffing becomes firm (approximately 45 mins).

Serve with Chicken or Beef Gravy on page 202.

Corn Salad (Raw)

2 CUPS CORN KERNELS

1 RED BELL PEPPER, CHOPPED

1 AVOCADO, PEELED AND CHOPPED

½ CUP CILANTRO

UP TO ½ TEASPOON SEA SALT

¼ CUP COLD-PRESSED, EXTRA-VIRGIN OLIVE OIL

2 TABLESPOONS LEMON JUICE

1. Combine all ingredients in a medium mixing bowl.

2. Stir to blend, then serve.

Fluffy Mashed Potatoes

3 LARGE RUSSET POTATOES
½ CUP EXTRA VIRGIN OLIVE OIL
1 GARLIC CLOVE, CHOPPED
2 TEASPOONS DRIED, CRUSHED
   THYME LEAVES
½ TEASPOON SALT
½ TEASPOON BLACK PEPPER
UP TO 1 CUP WARM WATER, CHICKEN
   BROTH, OR VEGETABLE BROTH

1. Peel and wash potatoes and cut into thirds.

2. Boil potatoes until soft. Drain excess water. Place in a large mixing bowl and set aside.

3. Combine olive oil, garlic, thyme, salt, and pepper in a small saucepan. Simmer over low heat. Stir constantly until brown.

4. Add garlic mixture to potatoes. Mash with a large fork until lumpy.

5. Add ½ cup of warm water or broth. Mix with an electric mixer at low speed.

6. Increase the mixer speed to medium. Mix and add liquid until potatoes are light and fluffy.

Top with Fried Onion Topping on page 201.

Gazpacho (Raw)

SOUP
1 CUP WATER
½ CUP COLD-PRESSED OLIVE OIL
4 LARGE TOMATOES
1 LARGE GARLIC CLOVE
5 FRESH BASIL LEAVES
2 CUPS FRESH CILANTRO LEAVES
½ TEASPOON SEA SALT

TOPPING CHOICES
RED BELL PEPPER. CHOPPED
RED ONION, CHOPPED
CUBED AVOCADO
SHREDDED CARROTS
SLICED SCALLIONS

1. Combine all soup ingredients in a blender and blend until smooth.

2. Pour into individual bowls and add toppings to each.

3. Serve at room temperature or chilled.

Gazpacho can be eaten as a soup or used as a dip for vegetables or corn tortillas.

Hummus (Raw)

½ CUP SESAME OR PUMPKIN BUTTER
  FROM PAGE 203
1 SMALL ZUCCHINI
4 LARGE BLACK OLIVES, PITTED
4 LARGE GREEN OLIVES, PITTED
1 SMALL GARLIC CLOVE
2 TEASPOONS GROUND CUMIN
3 TABLESPOONS COLD-PRESSED
  OLIVE OIL
½ TEASPOON SEA SALT
JUICE OF 1 SMALL LEMON

1. Combine all ingredients in a blender.

2. Blend at high speed until thick and creamy.

Serve as a dip with fresh carrot sticks or tortilla chips.

Korean Cucumber Kimchee (Raw)

10 KIRBY CUCUMBERS (ALSO CALLED
    PICKLING CUCUMBERS)
½ CUP SEA SALT
6 SMALL GARLIC CLOVES, MINCED
4 WHOLE SCALLIONS, SLICED
2 TABLESPOONS FRESH GINGER,
    PEELED AND FINELY CHOPPED
¼ CUP SESAME OIL
¼ CUP RAW SESAME SEEDS
1 TEASPOON RAW AGAVE NECTAR
CRUSHED RED PEPPER TO TASTE

1. Wash and slice cucumbers. Place in a large bowl.

2. Pour salt over cucumbers. Toss with your hands until the salt is evenly distributed.

3. Cover with a cloth. Set aside at room temperature for at least 2 hours. Salt will draw moisture out of the cucumbers.

4. Use a strainer to rinse the cucumbers under cold, running water. Keep rinsing until all the salt is removed. Taste frequently to test.

5. Squeeze water from the cucumbers using your hands. Remove as much water as possible. Cucumbers will be limp.

6. Place cucumbers in a medium bowl and add garlic, scallions, ginger, sesame seeds, and sesame oil. Toss with a fork.

7. Add agave and crushed red pepper to taste. Toss.

8. Chill and serve.

Serve with spiral corn pasta tossed in sesame oil.

Korean Dumpling Soup

BASE

8 CUPS OF CHICKEN OR BEEF BROTH
1 TABLESPOON DARK SESAME OIL
4 SCALLIONS, CHOPPED
1 TABLESPOON MINCED GINGER
¼ CUP ROASTED SESAME SEEDS
SALT AND GROUND BLACK PEPPER TO
TASTE
CRUSHED RED PEPPER TO TASTE
SALT TO TASTE

DUMPLING

½ CUP BUCKWHEAT FLOUR
2 TABLESPOONS TAPIOCA FLOUR
½ TEASPOON SALT
1 TABLESPOON PALM OIL
SHORTENING
¼ CUP WATER

1. Combine the soup base ingredients in a large pot. Bring to a boil. Reduce the temperature to low and let simmer for 20 mins.

2. Meanwhile, prepare dumplings. Stir together flours and salt in a small bowl. Add shortening and water. Stir until a sticky dough forms. Set aside until the soup has cooked for 20 mins.

3. Remove the lid from the soup pot while continuing to simmer. Scoop 1 tablespoon of dough. Use floured hands (buckwheat) to flatten the dough to ¼-inch thickness.

4. Drop the dough into the simmering soup. Repeat until all of the dough has been used and turn off heat. Dumplings should cook for no more than 2 mins.

5. Serve immediately.

Makes 4 to 5 servings. For those who are not allergic to rice, dumpling can be replaced with store-bought rice dumplings found in Asian marketplaces.

Korean Seasoned Spinach (Raw)

1   LB BABY SPINACH LEAVES,
     THOROUGHLY WASHED
5   GARLIC CLOVES, MINCED
3   WHOLE SCALLIONS, SLICED
1   TABLESPOON FRESH GINGER,
     PEELED AND FINELY CHOPPED
1   TEASPOON AGAVE NECTAR
½   TEASPOON SEA SALT
3   TABLESPOONS SESAME OIL
3   TABLESPOONS ROASTED SESAME
     SEEDS
CRUSHED RED PEPPER TO TASTE

1. Bring 5 cups of water to a full boil in a large pot.

2. Drop spinach into water for 30 seconds. Drain promptly into a strainer.

3. Run spinach under cold water to cool completely.

4. Use your hands to squeeze remaining water from the spinach. Spinach will be limp.

5. Place spinach in a small mixing bowl. Use your hands to toss and loosen the leaves.

6. Add garlic, scallions, ginger, agave, salt, sesame seeds, and sesame oil. Mix well with a fork.

7. If desired, add crushed red pepper to taste.

Serve with steamed quinoa or corn spaghetti tossed in sesame oil.

Guacamole (Raw)

2 LARGE AVOCADOES, PEELED
½ TEASPOON SALT
1 LARGE TOMATO, DICED
2 SCALLIONS, CHOPPED
1 SMALL RED ONION, CHOPPED
½ CUP FRESH CILANTRO LEAVES,
    CHOPPED
JUICE OF 1 SMALL LIME

1. Place avocadoes and salt in a medium bowl. Mash with a fork until smooth.

2. Mix in tomatoes, scallions, onions, and cilantro with the avocado.

3. Squeeze fresh lime juice over top.

Chill and serve with organic corn tortilla chips.

Potato Salad

3 LARGE RUSSET POTATOES
½ CUP CORN OR SAFFLOWER OIL
¼ CUP APPLE CIDER VINEGAR
1 STRIP OF UNCURED PORK OR
   TURKEY BACON, COOKED AND
   CHOPPED
½ CUP GREEN PEPPER, FINELY
   CHOPPED
½ CUP CELERY, FINELY CHOPPED
1 TABLESPOON ONION, FINELY
   CHOPPED
SALT AND PEPPER TO TASTE
PAPRIKA AND SCALLIONS TO GARNISH

1. Peel potatoes. Wash and cut into bite-sized cubes.

2. Boil potatoes until slightly soft, not mushy. Drain and place in a large bowl. Cool completely.

3. Add oil, vinegar, bacon, green pepper, celery, and onion.

4. Stir gently with a large spoon until blended. Add salt and pepper to taste.

5. Garnish with paprika and chopped scallions.

6. Chill and serve.

Quinoa Mexican Style

1 CUP QUINOA
2 ½ CUPS WATER OR UNSALTED
   CHICKEN BROTH
3 GARLIC CLOVES, MINCED
¼ CUP TOMATO, CHOPPED
¼ CUP CORN KERNELS
¼ CUP CELERY, CHOPPED
½ TEASPOON SALT
1 TABLESPOON GROUND CUMIN
½ TEASPOON CHILI POWDER
   (OPTIONAL)
1 CUP QUINOA SEEDS

1. In a medium pot add broth or water and stir in vegetables and seasonings. Bring to a boil and reduce heat to a simmer.

2. Stir in quinoa seeds. Cover and simmer over very low heat until water is absorbed and quinoa is done, (approximately 20-30 mins).

3. Remove lid and fluff with a spoon.

4. Cool slightly, garnish with cilantro, and serve with grilled meat, tacos or Enchiladas on page 41.

Quinoa Stir-Fry

2 TABLESPOONS LIGHT SESAME OIL
1 STALK OF CELERY, CHOPPED
¼ CUP RED BELL PEPPER, CHOPPED
¼ CUP CARROT, PEELED AND
   CHOPPED
1 SCALLION, CHOPPED
½ TEASPOON SALT
1 BOK CHOY STALK, CHOPPED
2 GARLIC CLOVES, MINCED
1 TEASPOON GINGER POWDER
2 CUPS COOKED QUINOA
¼ CUP ROASTED SESAME SEEDS

1. In a large pan or wok, heat sesame oil over medium heat. Add celery, bell pepper, carrot, scallion and salt. Stir constantly until vegetables are soft (approximately 7 mins). Reduce heat to low.

2. Add bok choy, garlic, and ginger powder. Stir while cooking until garlic is soft (approximately 3 mins).

3. Add cooked quinoa and stir until quinoa is warm and blended into the vegetable mixture.

4. Remove from heat. Serve warm. Sprinkle 1 pinch of sesame seeds over each serving.

Meat option: before adding vegetables in step 1, add five thin strips of beef sirloin or boneless, skinless chicken breast to heated sesame oil. Cook and stir until meat is done and continue with step 1.

Quinoa Salad with Sweet Chili Sauce

2   CUPS COOKED QUINOA
1   RED BELL PEPPER, CHOPPED
2   SCALLIONS, MINCED
1   MEDIUM CARROT, SHREDDED
¼   CUP THAI SWEET CHILI SAUCE
½   CUP TOASTED PUMPKIN SEEDS,
    COARSELY CHOPPED
2   TABLESPOONS APPLE CIDER
    VINEGAR
SALT TO TASTE

1. Combine all ingredients a large bowl. Toss until blended.

2. Serve either chilled or at room temperature.

Rosemary Potatoes

5 MEDIUM-SIZED RED OR GOLDEN
  POTATOES
½ CUP EXTRA VIRGIN OLIVE OIL
3 GARLIC CLOVES, MINCED
½ TEASPOON DRIED, CRUSHED
  ROSEMARY LEAVES
½ TEASPOON SALT
1 TEASPOON BLACK PEPPER

1. Preheat oven to 325°F.

2. Cover a cookie sheet with aluminum foil and set aside.

3. Wash potatoes thoroughly. Slice into wedges.

4. Combine potatoes, olive oil, garlic, rosemary, salt, and pepper in a large bowl.

5. Stir thoroughly with a large spoon.

6. Spread seasoned potatoes over the cookie sheet.

7. Place cookie sheet on the middle rack of the oven.

8. Bake for approximately 40 mins or until potatoes are soft when pricked with a fork.

Sausage-Chicken Gumbo

¼ CUP EXTRA VIRGIN OLIVE OIL
1 SMALL ONION, CHOPPED
4 GARLIC CLOVES, MINCED
1 TABLESPOON CRUSHED THYME
½ TEASPOON EACH OF SALT AND
  GROUND BLACK PEPPER
5 CUPS CHICKEN OR BEEF BROTH
1 LARGE TOMATO, DICED
1 STALK OF CELERY, CHOPPED
2 CUPS FROZEN, CUT OKRA
1 CUP FROZEN BLACK EYED PEAS
5 CHICKEN WING DRUMMETS
2 CUPS KIELBASA SAUSAGE OR
  OTHER COOKED, SMOKED SAUSAGE.

THICKENER
1 CUP WATER
¼ CUP LIGHT BUCKWHEAT FLOUR

1. Pour olive oil into a medium pot. Sauté the onion over medium heat until soft. Add garlic and stir until the garlic is light brown.

2. Stir in thyme, salt, pepper, and broth. Increase the temperature to bring to a simmer.

3. Add all other ingredients (except thickener ingredients) and stir. Cover and continue to simmer 30-35 mins or until chicken is fully cooked.

4. Meanwhile, prepare thickener. Combine water and flour in a small bowl. Stir with a whisk until blended. Slowly pour the mixture into the simmering pot while stirring constantly for one minute.

5. Let cool slightly before serving. Serve over steamed quinoa.

Savory Potatoes

2 MEDIUM RUSSET POTATOES, SLICED ¼ INCH THICK, WITH SKIN
1 CUP CHICKEN BROTH
½ TEASPOON LIGHT BUCKWHEAT FLOUR
1½ TEASPOONS RUBBED SAGE
½ TEASPOON GROUND BLACK PEPPER
½ TEASPOON SALT (OPTIONAL DEPENDING ON SALTINESS OF BROTH)
1 TEASPOON EACH ONION POWDER AND GARLIC POWDER
2 TABLESPOONS EXTRA-VIRGIN OLIVE OIL
¼ CUP BACON BITS

1. Preheat oven to 400°F.

2. Place potatoes, overlapping on each end, in a glass baking dish (with a cover). Set aside.

3. In a small bowl, combine broth and buckwheat flour. Stir with a whisk until flour is dissolved. Add all other ingredients and stir until blended.

4. Pour the broth mixture over the potatoes. Cover tightly and bake 30 mins. Uncover and bake an additional 20 mins.

5. Cool slightly and serve.

Makes 3 to 4 servings.

Stuffed Baked Potato

2   LARGE RUSSET POTATOES
¼   CUP OLIVE OIL
½   TEASPOON SALT
1   GARLIC CLOVE, MINCED
½   SMALL ONION, MINCED
ADDITIONAL OLIVE OIL

1. Preheat oven to 400°F.

2. Lightly oil potatoes. Place directly on the oven rack and bake for 1 hour. Turn halfway through cooking. Let cool completely.

3. Meanwhile, combine ¼ cup olive oil, salt, onions, and garlic in a small saucepan. Cook over low setting until very soft. Turn off heat and set aside.

4. Once cooled, slice potatoes in half, lengthwise. Scoop out potato filling, keeping shells intact. Place the filling in a small bowl.

5. Add the cooked onion mixture to the potato filling. Mix with an electric mixer on low speed until the mixture is smooth. Add additional olive oil by the teaspoon to loosen, if needed.

6. Spoon the potato mix back into the shells.

7. Bake at 400°F until tops of potatoes are crusty and light brown, approximately 30 mins.

    Sprinkle with bacon bits or chopped scallions. Serve warm.

Simple Korean Stew

1 TABLESPOON EXTRA VIRGIN OLIVE
  OIL
½ POUND SIRLOIN BEEF CUBES
8 CUPS WATER
1 SMALL POTATO, PEELED AND CUBED
2 SCALLIONS, SLICED
1 SMALL ONION, SLICED
2 TABLESPOONS MINCED GINGER
4 GARLIC CLOVES, MINCED
1 SMALL ZUCCHINI, SLICED INTO
  CIRCLES
4 BOK CHOY LEAVES, SLICED
½ CUP ROASTED SESAME SEEDS
SALT, PEPPER, CRUSHED RED PEPPER
  TO TASTE

1. In a large pot, heat olive oil to medium and cook the beef until brown on all sides.

2. Add water, potatoes, scallion, onion, ginger, and garlic. Bring to a very low simmer and cover. Cook 45 mins or until the beef is thoroughly cooked.

3. Open the lid and add zucchini, bok choy, ¼ cup of sesame seeds and seasonings to taste. Cover and simmer 5 mins.

4. Pour into serving bowls and use finger tips to crush remaining sesame seeds into individual bowls.

Makes 4 to 5 servings.

Slow Cooker Chicken Chili Soup

SOUP
2   BONELESS, SKINLESS CHICKEN
    BREASTS CUT INTO CUBES
3   CUPS TOMATO, CUBED
½   CUP CORN KERNELS
3   CUPS CHICKEN BROTH
1   ONION, MINCED
2   GARLIC CLOVES, MINCED
1   TABLESPOON GROUND BLACK
    PEPPER
1   TABLESPOON CUMIN POWDER
SALT TO TASTE
1   CUP CILANTRO, CHOPPED

TOPPING
JUICE FROM 1 FRESH LIME
TORTILLA CHIPS
SLICED AVOCADO

1. Place all soup ingredients in a crock pot. Stir until well blended.

2. Set temperature to high heat, cover, and cook for 5-6 hours.

3. Pour into bowls and top with tortilla chip pieces, avocado, and lime juice.

Steamed Quinoa or Buckwheat with Veggies
(a yummy substitute for rice pilaf)

2 TABLESPOONS OLIVE OIL
½ CUP EACH OF CELERY, ONION, CARROT, AND GREEN PEPPER, CHOPPED
2 CUPS WATER OR BROTH
1 CUP WHOLE QUINOA SEEDS OR ROASTED BUCKWHEAT SEEDS
UP TO ½ TEASPOON SALT

1. Heat olive oil over low heat in a medium pot.

2. Add all vegetables and salt. Stir frequently. Cook until brown.

3. Add water or broth to the pot. Increase heat, bringing the liquid to a boil.

4. Add quinoa or buckwheat seeds and stir until all ingredients are well blended.

5. Reduce heat to a low simmer. Cover tightly with a lid. Let simmer for 10 mins or until water has soaked into the seeds.

6. Fluff with a fork prior to serving.

Sweet Potato Casserole

2   LARGE SWEET POTATOES (OR YAMS), COOKED
½   CUP CORN OR SAFFLOWER OIL
2   TEASPOONS GROUND CINNAMON
½   TEASPOON GROUND NUTMEG
2   TABLESPOONS LIGHT BROWN SUGAR
½   TEASPOON SALT (OPTIONAL)
UP TO 1 CUP WARM WATER
2   CUPS MINIATURE MARSHMALLOWS

1. Preheat the oven to 400°F.

2. Place potatoes in a large mixing bowl. Add oil, cinnamon, nutmeg, brown sugar, and salt to the potatoes. Mash with a large fork until lumpy.

3. Add ½ cup of warm water. Mix with an electric mixer at low speed.

4. Increase the mixer speed to medium. Add water by the tablespoon until potatoes are light and fluffy.

5. Pour potatoes into a baking dish and spread marshmallows evenly over top.

6. Bake for approximately 15-20 mins or until marshmallows appear slightly brown.

Sweet Potato Fries

1 LARGE SWEET POTATO, PEELED IF
  DESIRED
1 TABLESPOON OLIVE OIL
½ TEASPOON EACH OF GARLIC
  POWDER AND SALT
PINCH OF GROUND NUTMEG (OPTIONAL)

1. Preheat oven to 400°F.

2. Wash and pat dry the sweet potato. Cut into slices and place in a medium mixing bowl.

3. Add oil and seasonings. Stir until blended.

4. Place the slices in a single layer, on a non-stick baking dish. Bake 30-40 mins until potatoes are light brown on the edges.

Thai Coconut Soup (Raw)

4 CUPS COCONUT WATER
1 SMALL GARLIC CLOVE
2 TABLESPOONS OLIVE OIL
1 TABLESPOON FRESH GINGER,
 FINELY CHOPPED
2 CHERRY TOMATOES
¼ CUP GREEN PEPPER, CHOPPED
JUICE OF 1 LARGE LIME
¼ CUP EACH OF FRESH BASIL,
 CILANTRO LEAVES,AND
 LEMONGRASS, CHOPPED
SLICED MUSHROOMS (OPTIONAL)
SALT TO TASTE

1. Blend all ingredients in a blender until smooth. Serve at room temperature or heat very slightly if desired. Top with sliced mushrooms if desired.

Vegetable Stir-Fry

5   LARGE MUSHROOMS, SLICED
1   LARGE ONION, SLICED
1   LARGE RED PEPPER, SLICED
½   LARGE ORANGE OR YELLOW
    PEPPER, SLICED
½   LARGE GREEN PEPPER, SLICED
½   LB FRESH BROCCOLI CROWNS
2   TABLESPOONS FRESH GINGER,
    PEELED AND FINELY CHOPPED
2   TABLESPOONS ROASTED SESAME
    SEEDS
¾   CUP EXTRA VIRGIN OLIVE OIL OR
    ROASTED SESAME OIL
SALT TO TASTE

1. Combine all ingredients in a large mixing bowl. Stir until oil is distributed.

2. Preheat a large cast-iron skillet or wok to high temperature. Do not add extra oil.

3. Add vegetables to the skillet or wok. Toss frequently for 2 mins. For softer vegetables, cook for 5 mins.

4. Serve immediately.

Serve with grilled chicken.

Zesty Pasta Salad

3 CUPS SPIRAL CORN PASTA
1 MEDIUM CARROT, PEELED AND
   CHOPPED
1 SMALL GREEN PEPPER, CHOPPED
1 CUP BROCCOLI CROWNS, CHOPPED
SLICED GRILLED CHICKEN (OPTIONAL)

DRESSING
1 PACKET DRY ITALIAN SALAD
   DRESSING MIX
½ CUP CORN OR SAFFLOWER OIL
½ CUP RAW CIDER VINEGAR

1. Boil pasta until cooked. Drain and rinse with cold water. Set aside.

2. Combine dressing mix, oil, and vinegar in a large mixing bowl. Whisk until blended.

3. Add pasta, vegetables, and chicken. Toss until blended.

4. Chill and serve.

"I may have been born different and misunderstood from birth, but
I know there is a place for me, somewhere in this universe."
—Alyson Bradley, AsPlanet—Alternative Spectrum

Wholesome Breads

Apple Bread

1   CUP QUINOA FLOUR
1   CUP LIGHT BUCKWHEAT FLOUR
2   TABLESPOONS BAKING POWDER
    (ALUMINUM-FREE)
1   TABLESPOON GROUND CINNAMON
¼   CUP EVAPORATED CANE JUICE (UP
    TO ¼ CUP MORE, IF DESIRED)
¼   TEASPOON SALT
1   CUP CHOPPED, PEELED APPLE
    (GALA APPLE RECOMMENDED)
1   CUP UNSWEETENED APPLESAUCE
½   CUP CORN OR SAFFLOWER OIL
2   CUPS WATER

1. Preheat oven to 400°F.

2. Stir together all dry ingredients in a medium bowl.

3. Add wet ingredients (including the apple) and stir.

4. Pour the batter into a glass or non-stick 9x5 loaf pan (at least 2 inches in height). Bake 40-45 mins or until the top is crusty and golden brown.

5. Cool completely to allow bread to settle before slicing.

Banana Bread

1 CUP QUINOA FLOUR
1 CUP LIGHT BUCKWHEAT FLOUR
2 TABLESPOONS BAKING POWDER
(ALUMINUM-FREE)
1 TABLESPOON GROUND CINNAMON
¼ CUP EVAPORATED CANE JUICE (UP
TO ¼ CUP MORE, IF DESIRED)
¼ TEASPOON SALT
1 CUP VERY RIPE, MASHED BANANA
1 CUP UNSWEETENED APPLESAUCE
1½ CUPS WATER
½ CUP CORN OR SAFFLOWER OIL
1 TABLESPOON GLUTEN-FREE
VANILLA EXTRACT (OPTIONAL)

1. Preheat oven to 400°F.

2. Stir together all dry ingredients in a medium bowl.

3. Add wet ingredients (including the banana) and stir.

4. Pour the batter into a glass or non-stick 9x5 loaf pan (at least 2 inches in height). Bake 40-45 mins or until the top is crusty and golden brown.

5. Cool completely, allowing the bread to settle before slicing.

Cornbread Muffins

2 CUPS CORNMEAL

2 TABLESPOONS LIGHT BUCKWHEAT
FLOUR

OR

1 TABLESPOON DARK BUCKWHEAT
FLOUR

1 TABLESPOON FLAXSEED MEAL
(OPTIONAL)

1 TABLESPOON BAKING POWDER
(ALUMINUM-FREE)

½ TEASPOON SALT

¼ CUP EVAPORATED CANE JUICE

½ CUP UNSWEETENED APPLESAUCE

½ CUP CORN OR SAFFLOWER OIL

1 CUP WATER

1. Preheat oven to 400°F.

2. In a medium bowl, combine dry ingredients and stir.

3. Add wet ingredients and stir until blended.

4. Spoon the batter into a non-stick muffin pan or non-stick 8-inch baking dish.

5. Bake 20-25 mins for muffins (25-30 mins if using baking dish) or until center is firm when pressed.

Serve with Chunky Red Bean Chili on page 12. Also try with warm Sesame or Pumpkin "Butter" on page 203 or with fruit jam as a spread.

Ella's Italian Crackers (Raw)

1 CUP GOLDEN FLAX SEEDS
½ CUP EACH OF SWEET ONION AND
   RED BELL PEPPER
1 CUP CHOPPED TOMATOES
1½ TABLESPOONS FRESH LEMON JUICE
½ GARLIC CLOVE
1 STALK OF CELERY
1 TEASPOON EACH OF DRIED BASIL,
   OREGANO, AND SEA SALT

1. Use an Excalibur food dehydrator or preheat an oven to the lowest setting with the door ajar.

2. Place all ingredients in a food processor and process until uniform. Seeds will remain whole. Turn off the food processor, scrape down the sides, and process again. Entire processing time should take no longer than one minute.

3. Use a spatula to spread the mixture evenly over a teflex sheet (non-stick dehydrator sheet) or use a 14x14-inch sheet of parchment paper for the oven.

4. Place the teflex sheet on a dehydrator tray or place the parchment paper on a baking tray.

5. Place in the dehydrator at 105°F or in the oven with the door ajar for five hours.

6. Remove the tray from the dehydrator or oven. Place the teflex or parchment sheet on the counter and score the crackers to your desired size.

Hushpuppies

1 CUP CORNMEAL
2 TABLESPOONS LIGHT BUCKWHEAT
  FLOUR
1½ TEASPOONS BAKING POWDER
  (ALUMINUM-FREE)
½ TEASPOON EACH SALT AND GROUND
  BLACK PEPPER
½ TEASPOON EACH GARLIC POWDER
  AND ONION POWDER
¼ CUP CORN OR SAFFLOWER OIL
½ CUP + 1 TABLESPOON WATER
OIL FOR DEEP FRYING

1. Preheat oil in a deep fryer. Line a plate with paper towels.

2. In a medium bowl, combine dry ingredients and stir.

3. Add wet ingredients and stir until well blended.

4. Scoop 1 tablespoon of batter with a spoon. Use another spoon to slide the batter into the hot oil. Cook 5 to 7 hushpuppies at a time until fully cooked (approximately 20-30 seconds). Remove carefully and place on lined plate to drain oil.

5. Continue until all batter has been used. Cool slightly before serving.

Italian-Style Breadcrumbs

3 CUPS QUINOA FLAKES
½ CUP FLAXSEED MEAL
1 TABLESPOON GARLIC POWDER
½ TEASPOON SALT
1 TABLESPOON DRIED, CRUSHED BASIL
1 TABLESPOON DRIED, CRUSHED OREGANO

1. Combine all ingredients in a blender and blend on low speed until crumbly.

2. Store breadcrumbs in a container and cover tightly until ready for use.

3. Store in a cool, dry place.

Use in Meatloaf and Meatballs with Sweet Glaze recipes.

Cardamom Zucchini Bread

2 CUPS LIGHT BUCKWHEAT FLOUR

2 TABLESPOONS BAKING POWDER (ALUMINUM-FREE)

¼ CUP EVAPORATED CANE JUICE (UP TO 2 TABLESPOONS MORE, IF DESIRED)

¼ TEASPOON SALT

2 TABLESPOONS GROUND CARDAMOM

1 CUP CHOPPED ZUCCHINI

½ CUP COARSELY CHOPPED, RAW PUMPKIN SEEDS (OPTIONAL)

¾ CUP UNSWEETENED APPLESAUCE

2 CUPS WATER

½ CUP CORN OR SAFFLOWER OIL

1. Preheat oven to 400°F.

2. In a medium mixing bowl, combine dry ingredients, including zucchini and pumpkin seeds, if used. Stir until well blended.

3. Add wet ingredients and stir well.

4. Pour into a glass or non-stick 9x5 loaf pan (at least 2 inches in height) and bake 40-45 mins or until top is golden brown and crusty.

5. Cool completely to allow bread to set before slicing.

Peachy Cornbread

1 CORNBREAD MUFFIN RECIPE FROM
   PAGE 117
1 16-OUNCE CAN OF SLICED PEACHES,
   DRAINED

1. Preheat oven to 400°F.

2. Line the bottom of a 9-inch pie pan with peach slices. Set aside.

3. Prepare batter from Cornbread Muffin recipe from page 117.

4. Pour the batter evenly over the peaches.

5. Bake 30 mins or until the top is firm when touched.

6. Cool slightly before serving.

Pumpkin Bread

2   CUPS LIGHT BUCKWHEAT FLOUR
2   TABLESPOONS BAKING POWDER
    (ALUMINUM-FREE)
¼   CUP EVAPORATED CANE JUICE
    (UP TO 2 TABLESPOONS MORE, IF
    DESIRED)
¼   TEASPOON SALT
2   TEASPOONS PUMPKIN PIE SPICE
    (BY MCCORMICK) OR 1 TABLESPOON
    GROUND CINNAMON
½   CUP UNSWEETENED APPLESAUCE
1   CUP FULLY COOKED, MASHED
    PUMPKIN
½   CUP CORN OR SAFFLOWER OIL
2   CUPS WATER
½   CUP RAISINS (OPTIONAL)

1. Preheat oven to 400°F.

2. Combine dry ingredients (including raisins, if desired) in a large bowl and stir until blended.

3. Add wet ingredients and mix well.

4. Pour batter into a glass or non-stick 9x5 loaf pan (at least 2 inches in height). Bake 40-45 mins or until the top is golden brown and crusty.

5. Cool completely before serving to allow bread to settle.

6. For a festive holiday taste, pour Orange Glaze recipe from page 209 over the top of cooled bread.

Veggie Cornbread Muffins

1 CORNBREAD MUFFINS RECIPE FROM
   PAGE 117
1 TABLESPOON EACH FINELY
   CHOPPED ZUCCHINI, GREEN BELL
   PEPPER AND RED BELL PEPPER
¼ CUP CORN KERNELS

1. Preheat oven to 400°F.

2. Prepare Cornbread Muffins batter. Add zucchini, peppers, and corn with the wet ingredients. Stir well to blend.

3. Pour batter into a non-stick muffin pan. Bake 15-20 mins, until muffins are firm and crusty.

4. Cool slightly before serving.

Wholesome Fruit and Seed Bread

1   CUP QUINOA FLOUR
¼   CUP LIGHT BUCKWHEAT FLOUR OR
    AMARANTH FLOUR
2   TABLESPOONS TAPIOCA FLOUR
¼   CUP MILLET FLOUR
¼   CUP FLAXSEED MEAL
1   TABLESPOON BAKING POWDER
    (ALUMINUM-FREE)
¼   CUP EVAPORATED CANE JUICE
½   TEASPOON SALT
1   TABLESPOON GROUND CINNAMON
½   CUP DRIED CRANBERRIES
5   DRIED, PITTED DATES, CHOPPED
    (OPTIONAL)
½   CUP RAW, HULLED PUMPKIN SEEDS
½   CUP UNSWEETENED APPLESAUCE
1   CUP WATER OR APPLE JUICE
¼   CUP CORN OR SAFFLOWER OIL

1. Preheat oven to 400°F.

2. In a medium mixing bowl, combine dry ingredients, including the seeds and fruit. Stir to blend.

3. Add wet ingredients and stir until well blended.

4. Pour into a glass or non-stick 9x5 loaf pan (at least 2 inches in height). Bake 35-40 mins. Top will appear golden brown.

5. Cool completely before slicing to allow the bread to set.

Note: this bread is semi-sweet. For sweeter bread, add up to ¼ cup more evaporated cane juice.

"Parent's Job=prepare the child for the world.
Parent of autistic child's job=prepare the world for the child."
—Stuart Duncan, "Autism from a Father's Point of View"

Breakfast Items

The Autism Cookbook

Apple Cinnamon Quinoa

1½ CUPS WATER
½ CUP APPLE, PEELED AND CHOPPED
½ TEASPOON SALT
2 TABLESPOONS AGAVE NECTAR
½ CUP QUINOA FLAKES
GROUND CINNAMON TO TASTE

TOPPING CHOICES
KIWI FRUIT
RASPBERRIES
RAISINS
SLICED BANANAS
PURE MAPLE SYRUP

1. In a medium pot, bring water to a boil. Stir in apples, salt, and agave nectar.

2. Reduce heat to medium and let simmer for 2 mins. Stir in quinoa flakes and cinnamon. Reduce heat to low and stir for 1 minute.

3. Remove from heat and allow the cereal to thicken. Serve warm.

4. If desired, top with raisins, sliced bananas,kiwi fruit, raspberries, and/or pure maple syrup.

Apple Salad (Raw)

1 LARGE GRANNY SMITH APPLE, CUT
   INTO BITE-SIZED PIECES
1 TABLESPOON COLD PRESSED,
   EXTRA-VIRGIN OLIVE OIL
¼ TEASPOON SEA SALT (OPTIONAL)
2 TABLESPOONS FLAXSEED MEAL
¼ CUP RAW, HULLED PUMPKIN SEEDS
¼ CUP RAISINS
RAW AGAVE NECTAR TO TASTE
   (OPTIONAL)

1. Combine all ingredients in a medium mixing bowl.

2. Stir until well blended and serve.

Banana-Blueberry Flax Muffins

1   CUP QUINOA FLOUR

2   TABLESPOONS LIGHT BUCKWHEAT
    FLOUR

¼   CUP FLAXSEED MEAL

1   TABLESPOON BAKING POWDER
    (ALUMINUM-FREE)

1   TEASPOON GROUND CINNAMON
    (RECOMMENDED)

¼   CUP EVAPORATED CANE JUICE

¼   TEASPOON SALT

½   CUP DRIED BLUEBERRIES

½   CUP VERY RIPE MASHED BANANA

¼   CUP CORN OR SAFFLOWER OIL

1   CUP WATER

1. Preheat oven to 400°F.

2. Stir together dry ingredients (including blueberries) in a medium bowl.

3. Add wet ingredients (including bananas) and stir until well blended.

4. Pour batter into a non-stick muffin pan and bake 20-25 mins, until muffins are golden brown.

5. Cool slightly before serving.

Makes 6 to 8 muffins, depending on muffin pan size.

Note: this bread is semi-sweet. For sweeter bread, add up to ¼ cup more evaporated cane juice.

Grits with Bacon

2 CUPS CHICKEN BROTH
½ TEASPOON SALT
½ TEASPOON GROUND BLACK PEPPER
¼ TEASPOON GARLIC POWDER
1 CUP QUICK GRITS
3 SLICES OF UNCURED PORK OR TURKEY BACON, COOKED AND CHOPPED

1. Combine chicken broth, salt, pepper, and garlic powder in a small pot. Bring to a boil and stir until salt is dissolved.

2. Add grits and reduce heat to low. Stir constantly until boiling stops.

3. Cover and cook over low heat until grits start to thicken (2-5 mins).

4. Crumble bacon over grits. Stir and serve warm.

Berry Breakfast Bars

2 CUPS RAW, HULLED PUMPKIN
  SEEDS OR SUNFLOWER SEEDS
¼ TEASPOON SEA SALT
½ CUP RAW, HULLED SESAME SEEDS
1 TEASPOON FLAXSEED MEAL
1 CUP DRIED CRANBERRIES
¼ CUP LEMON JUICE

1. Finely chop the pumpkin or sunflower seeds in a blender. Add salt, sesame seeds, and flaxseed meal. Pulse several times to blend.

2. Add cranberries and chop for approximately 30 seconds.

3. Pour mixture into a small bowl. Add lemon juice and stir until the mixture resembles a thick dough.

4. Press into a small square pan.

5. Slice and serve.

6. To store, stack each slice, separated by parchment paper. Store in an airtight container.

Blueberry Muffins

FLOUR OPTIONS
½ CUP QUINOA FLOUR
½ CUP LIGHT BUCKWHEAT FLOUR
OR
½ CUP QUINOA FLOUR
½ CUP WHOLE GRAIN AMARANTH
   FLOUR
OR
1 CUP LIGHT BUCKWHEAT FLOUR

1 TABLESPOON FLAXSEED MEAL
   (OPTIONAL)
1 TABLESPOON BAKING POWDER
   (ALUMINUM-FREE)
¼ CUP EVAPORATED CANE JUICE
¼ TEASPOON SALT
¼ CUP CORN OR SAFFLOWER OIL
¾ CUP WATER
½ CUP FRESH OR FROZEN
   BLUEBERRIES

1. Preheat oven to 400°F.

2. Combine dry ingredients in a medium bowl and stir.

3. Add water and oil, and stir with a spoon until well blended.

4. Very gently stir in blueberries.

5. Pour batter into a glass or non-stick muffin pan. Bake 20-25 mins, until muffins are golden brown.

6. Cool slightly before serving.

Note: this muffin recipe is semi-sweet. For sweeter muffins, add up to ¼ more evaporated cane juice.

Breakfast Kabobs

2 TABLESPOONS OLIVE OIL
1 MEDIUM POTATO CUBED, AND
   PEELED, IF DESIRED
½ TEASPOON EACH OF SALT, GARLIC
   POWDER, AND BLACK PEPPER
1 MEDIUM APPLE, CUBED
COOKED BREAKFAST SAUSAGE, CUT
   INTO BITE-SIZED PIECES

1. Preheat oven to 400°F.

2. In a medium bowl combine oil, potatoes, apples, and seasonings. Toss until well blended.

3. Place potatoes and apples on a non-stick baking pan and bake until potatoes and apples are soft and light brown. Let cool slightly.

4. On metal skewers, alternately place sausage, apples, and potatoes until the skewer is full.

Breakfast Sausage Patties

½ LB GROUND TURKEY
1 TEASPOON EACH OF DRIED, FINELY
  GROUND SAGE LEAVES, THYME
  LEAVES, AND ROSEMARY LEAVES
1 TEASPOON ALLSPICE SEASONING
1 TEASPOON GARLIC POWDER
1 TEASPOON SALT
1 TEASPOON GROUND BLACK PEPPER
2 TABLESPOONS MOLASSES

1. Combine all ingredients in a large mixing bowl. Mix thoroughly until the meat is smooth.

2. For best flavor, cover tightly and marinate in the refrigerator for at least 2 hours.

3. Use your hands to form 2-inch round patties.

4. Heat a non-stick skillet to medium setting. Cook thoroughly on each side.

Home Fries

2 LARGE POTATOES
2 TABLESPOONS OLIVE OIL
½ CUP EACH OF CHOPPED ONION AND
   GREEN BELL PEPPER
½ TEASPOON EACH OF SALT AND
   GROUND BLACK PEPPER
¼ CUP WATER

1. Peel and cube the potatoes.

2. Heat olive oil in a large skillet to medium setting. Add potatoes, onion, green pepper, salt, and black pepper.

3. Sauté and stir until vegetables are soft. Stir in water and reduce heat to low setting.

4. Cover and let simmer until potatoes are soft.

Orange Essence Cranberry Muffins

FLOUR OPTIONS
½ CUP LIGHT BUCKWHEAT FLOUR
½ CUP QUINOA FLOUR
OR
½ CUP QUINOA FLOUR
½ CUP AMARANTH FLOUR

1 TABLESPOON BAKING POWDER
  (ALUMINUM-FREE)
¼ CUP EVAPORATED CANE JUICE
¼ TEASPOON SALT
2 TABLESPOONS DRIED OR FRESH
  ORANGE PEEL (MINCED)
½ CUP CRANBERRIES
¼ CUP CORN OR SAFFLOWER OIL
¾ CUP ORANGE JUICE

1. Preheat oven to 400°F.

2. In a medium mixing bowl, combine dry ingredients, including orange peel and cranberries. Stir to blend.

3. Add wet ingredients and stir until blended.

4. Pour batter into a non-stick muffin pan and bake 20-25 mins. Tops of muffins should be golden brown.

Pancakes and Waffles

FLOUR OPTIONS:

1   CUP QUINOA FLOUR
¼   CUP LIGHT BUCKWHEAT FLOUR
OR
1 CUP QUINOA FLOUR
¼ CUP WHOLE GRAIN AMARANTH
    FLOUR
OR
1¼ CUP LIGHT BUCKWHEAT FLOUR
OR
1   CUP QUINOA FLOUR
1   TABLESPOON TAPIOCA FLOUR

1   TABLESPOON BAKING POWDER
    (ALUMINUM-FREE)
¼   TEASPOON SALT
1   TABLESPOON FLAXSEED MEAL
    (RECOMMENDED)
¼   CUP CORN OR SAFFLOWER OIL
1¼ CUP WATER (UP TO ¼ CUP MORE
    WATER FOR THINNER PANCAKES OR
    WAFFLES)

RECOMMENDED ADD-INS:

1   TABLESPOON GLUTEN-FREE
    VANILLA EXTRACT
1   TEASPOON GROUND CINNAMON
½   CUP DRIED CRANBERRIES, DRIED
    BLUEBERRIES OR RAISINS
¼   TEASPOON GROUND NUTMEG
¼   CUP GROUND PUMPKIN SEED
½   CUP PEELED, CHOPPED APPLE

1. Combine dry ingredients and stir until blended.
2. Add wet ingredients and mix well.
3. Add desired add-ins and stir until incorporated into the batter.
4. For pancakes, set a non-stick griddle or frying pan to medium-low setting. Pour ¼ cup of batter onto the surface. Cook on each side until lightly golden (approximately 2 mins on each side).
5. For waffles, pour batter onto iron to fill the surface. Do not over-fill. Cook in accordance with waffle maker directions. See below for waffle maker recommendations.

Notes:

Sweetener is not added to this recipe because of our use of maple syrup when served. If desired, add sweetener of your choice such as 2 tablespoons of evaporated cane juice or 2 tablespoons agave nectar. The Quinoa-Amaranth flour combination will take 1-2 mins longer to cook.

2 brands of waffle makers were used in testing this recipe:

"Chefmate Belgian Waffle Maker," Model WM-77. Cooking time for this recipe is 6-7 mins using ½ cup of batter on each side of the waffle maker. Be sure to preheat.

"Oster Belgian Wafflemaker," Model 3883. Cooking time for this recipe is 5 mins on the two-dot heat setting, using ¾ cup of batter, applied to the center of the iron.

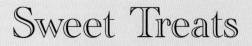

"Not everything that steps out of line and thus 'abnormal' must necessarily be 'inferior.'"
—Hans Asperger

Sweet Treats

The Autism Cookbook

Apple Fritters

CORN OR SAFFLOWER OIL FOR DEEP
FRYING
1   CUP LIGHT BUCKWHEAT FLOUR
1   TABLESPOON CORNMEAL
¼   CUP EVAPORATED CANE JUICE
½   TEASPOON SALT
1   TEASPOON BAKING POWDER
1   TEASPOON GROUND CINNAMON
1   CUP WATER
¼   CUP CORN OR SAFFLOWER OIL
2   PEELED APPLES, SLICED INTO
    ¼-INCH-THICK WEDGES

1. Preheat oil in deep fryer.

2. Stir together dry ingredients in a medium bowl. Stir in water and oil. Add apple wedges and stir until wedges are covered.

3. Pick up three apple wedges at a time with a slotted spoon. Place apple wedges into hot oil and fry until batter appears medium brown (approx. 60 seconds).

4. Remove with a spatula and drain excess oil.

5. Do not overcook. Cool completely before eating.

Brownies

GOOEY BROWNIES

1 CUP LIGHT OR DARK BUCKWHEAT FLOUR
½ CUP COCOA POWDER
1 TEASPOON BAKING SODA
½ CUP EVAPORATED CANE JUICE
½ TEASPOON SALT
½ CUP LIGHT BROWN SUGAR, PACKED
¾ CUP CORN OR SAFFLOWER OIL
½ CUP UNSWEETENED APPLESAUCE IF USING LIGHT BUCKWHEAT FLOUR
1 CUP UNSWEETENED APPLESAUCE IF USING DARK BUCKWHEAT FLOUR

NOTE: be sure to use baking soda and not baking powder

CAKE BROWNIES

1 CUP LIGHT BUCKWHEAT FLOUR
½ CUP COCOA POWDER
1 CUP EVAPORATED CANE JUICE
1 TABLESPOON BAKING POWDER
½ TEASPOON SALT
1¼ CUP WATER
¼ CUP CORN OR SAFFLOWER OIL
PUMPKIN SEEDS (OPTIONAL)

1. Preheat oven to 400°F.

2. In a medium mixing bowl, combine dry ingredients and stir.

3. Add wet ingredients and stir until a thick batter forms.

4. Pour the batter into an 8-inch baking dish. Spread evenly with a rubber spatula.

5. If desired, add pumpkin seed topping at this time.

6. For Gooey Brownies, bake 20-25 mins. Within a few mins after removing from oven, edges should become crusty and center should sink slightly when pressed with finger.

7. For Cake Brownies, bake 25-30 mins, until center is firm.

8. Cool before slicing and serve.

Suggested topping: Lightly roast ½ cup raw pumpkin seeds in a non-stick frying pan. Cool completely. Place in a blender with salt to taste (up to ½ teaspoon). Pulse several times until crumbly. Sprinkle over batter before baking
OR
Cool brownies completely and add chocolate glaze from page 209.

Berry Shortcake

1 CORNBREAD MUFFIN RECIPE FROM
  PAGE 117
OR
½ OF VANILLA CUPCAKE RECIPE FROM
  PAGE 185

3 CUPS FRESH OR FROZEN BERRIES
¼ CUP AGAVE NECTAR (OPTIONAL)
1 VANILLA FROSTING RECIPE FROM
  PAGE 210

1. If desired, soak berries in agave nectar and set aside (if using strawberries, slice berries in half before soaking).

2. Prepare Cornbread Muffin recipe OR half of Vanilla Cupcake recipe. Bake in a glass or non-stick 9-inch baking dish. Cool completely.

3. Top with berries and frosting. Slice and serve.

Carrot Cake

1   CUP LIGHT BUCKWHEAT FLOUR
1   CUP QUINOA FLOUR
2   TABLESPOONS TAPIOCA FLOUR
2   TABLESPOONS BAKING POWDER
      (ALUMINUM-FREE)
¼   CUP EVAPORATED CANE JUICE (UP
      TO ¼ CUP MORE, IF DESIRED)
½   TEASPOON SALT
1   TABLESPOON GROUND CINNAMON
1   CUP SHREDDED CARROT
½   CUP RAISINS (OPTIONAL)
½   CUP UNSWEETENED APPLESAUCE
½   CUP CORN OR SAFFLOWER OIL
1½ CUP WATER

1. Preheat oven to 400°F.

2. To shred carrots, place carrot in a blender and use the pulse button 8-10 times to chop.

3. Combine dry ingredients, including carrot and raisins, in a medium mixing bowl. Stir until blended.

4. Add wet ingredients and stir until a smooth batter forms.

5. Pour into a glass or non-stick 9-inch baking dish (at least 2 inches in height) or two 8-inch baking dishes (at least 1.5 inches in height).

6. Bake 25-30 mins, until center is firm.

7. Cool completely and top with White or Vanilla Glaze recipe from page 209.

Chocolate Cake

FLOUR OPTIONS
1   CUP LIGHT BUCKWHEAT FLOUR
OR
½   CUP DARK BUCKWHEAT FLOUR
½   CUP QUINOA FLOUR

1   TABLESPOON TAPIOCA FLOUR
1   TABLESPOON BAKING POWDER
    (ALUMINUM-FREE)
5   TABLESPOONS COCOA POWDER
    (REGULAR OR DARK)
½   CUP EVAPORATED CANE JUICE IF
    USING REGULAR COCOA (¾ CUP IF
    USING DARK COCOA)
¼   TEASPOON SALT
¼   CUP CORN OR SAFFLOWER OIL
1   CUP WATER IF USING LIGHT
    BUCKWHEAT FLOUR
1¼ CUP WATER IF USING FLOUR MIX
1   TABLESPOON GLUTEN-FREE
    VANILLA EXTRACT

1. Preheat oven to 400°F.

2. In a medium bowl, stir together dry ingredients.

3. Add wet ingredients and stir until a smooth batter forms.

4. Pour batter into a glass or non-stick 8-inch baking dish (at least 1.5 inches in height) or non-stick muffin pan. Bake 25-30 mins if using cake pan and 20-25 mins if using muffin pan. The center will be firm when done.

5. Cool completely and frost with Chocolate Frosting recipe from page 210.

Note: this recipe may be doubled to make two 8-inch cakes. One 9-inch cake is not recommended for this recipe.

Cinnamon-Raisin Cookies

1 CUP LIGHT BUCKWHEAT FLOUR
½ CUP QUINOA FLAKES
¼ CUP EVAPORATED CANE JUICE
½ CUP LIGHT BROWN SUGAR, PACKED
½ TEASPOON SALT
1 TABLESPOON GROUND CINNAMON
½ CUP RAISINS,(CHOPPED IN A
    BLENDER-OPTIONAL)
½ CUP WATER
¼ CUP CORN OR SAFFLOWER OIL

1. Preheat oven to 400°F.

2. Combine dry ingredients in a medium bowl, including raisins and stir.

3. Add wet ingredients and stir until a sticky dough forms.

4. Scoop 1 tablespoon of dough with a metal spoon and use a finger to slide the dough onto a non-stick or parchment paper-lined cookie sheet.

5. Continue placing dough 3 inches apart, until all of the dough has been used. Flatten slightly with fingertips.

6. Bake 12-15 mins. Cool slightly before serving

Cocoa Cookies

1 CUP LIGHT BUCKWHEAT FLOUR
½ TEASPOON BAKING SODA
¼ CUP UNSWEETENED COCOA
    POWDER (REGULAR OR DARK)
½ TEASPOON SALT
¾ CUP LIGHT BROWN SUGAR, PACKED
¼ CUP PALM OIL SHORTENING
½ CUP WATER
OPTIONAL: UP TO 2 TABLESPOONS
    EVAPORATED CANE JUICE FOR
    SWEETER COOKIES
OPTIONAL: ½ CUP GFCF CHOCOLATE
    CHIPS

1. Preheat oven to 400°F.

2. Combine dry ingredients in a medium bowl and stir. If using chocolate chips, add during this step.

3. Add shortening and water, and stir until a sticky dough forms.

4. Use a metal spoon to scoop a tablespoon of dough. Use finger to slide the dough onto a cookie sheet (non-stick or parchment-paper lined). Continue by placing the dough 3 inches apart until all of the dough has been used.

5. Bake 13-15 mins.

Coconut "Ice Cream" (Raw)

2 CUPS UNSWEETENED, SHREDDED
   COCONUT
¼ TEASPOON SALT
1 TABLESPOON GLUTEN-FREE
   VANILLA EXTRACT
UP TO 2 CUPS COCONUT WATER
ANY SWEETENER OF CHOICE TO TASTE

1. Combine coconut and salt in a blender. Blend on low speed.

2. After 1 minute, while still blending, open the lid and add vanilla extract and ¼ cup coconut water. Continue to add coconut water, ¼ cup at a time until a thick paste forms.

3. Turn blender off.

4. Add sweetener of choice. Pulse several times to blend.

5. Pour into a glass bowl, cover, and freeze. Serve frozen.

Crispy Cereal Treats

4 CUPS CEREAL OF YOUR
  CHOICE (CORN CHEX CEREAL
  RECOMMENDED)
4 CUPS MINIATURE MARSHMALLOWS
1 TABLESPOON CORN OR SAFFLOWER
  OIL FOR COATING

1. Place the cereal in a blender and pulse several times until coarsely chopped. Place in a bowl and set aside.

2. Place marshmallows in a large, microwave-safe bowl and cook in the microwave for 30 seconds.

3. Remove the bowl from the microwave and pour the chopped cereal into the hot marshmallows.

4. Use an oiled plastic spoon to stir the mixture until well blended.

5. Pour the mixture into an 8x8-inch square baking dish. Press and pack tightly with the oiled spoon–this may result in some empty space in the pan.

6. Let cool slightly and cut into squares.

7. Store in a cool dry place. Cereal treats will eventually harden. If desired, heat each square 10 seconds in the microwave to soften.

Crumb Cake

CRUMB TOPPING
- ¾ CUP LIGHT BUCKWHEAT FLOUR
- ½ CUP LIGHT BROWN SUGAR, PACKED
- 1 TABLESPOON CORN OR SAFFLOWER OIL
- 2 TABLESPOONS WATER

CAKE
- 1 CUP LIGHT BUCKWHEAT FLOUR
- 1 TABLESPOON BAKING POWDER (ALUMINUM-FREE)
- 1 TEASPOON GROUND CINNAMON
- ¼ CUP EVAPORATED CANE JUICE
- ¼ TEASPOON SALT
- ¼ CUP UNSWEETENED APPLESAUCE
- ¼ CUP CORN OR SAFFLOWER OIL
- 1 CUP WATER

1. Preheat oven to 400°F.

2. Prepare crumb topping. In a small bowl, combine flour and brown sugar. Stir to blend. Add in oil and water. Stir with a fork until the topping resembles thick cookie dough, separated into large clumps. Set aside.

3. Prepare cake. In a medium bowl, stir together dry ingredients. Add wet ingredients and stir until blended.

4. Pour batter into a glass or non-stick 8-inch baking dish (at least 1½ inches in height).

5. Spread topping evenly over the cake batter. Do not cover the batter completely.

6. Gently press the topping down about ¼ inch into the batter.

7. Bake 15-20 mins. Cool slightly.

Crusty Apple Cake

1 CUP QUINOA FLOUR
¼ CUP AMARANTH FLOUR
1 TABLESPOON MILLET FLOUR
1 TABLESPOON TAPIOCA FLOUR
1 TABLESPOON BAKING POWDER
½ TEASPOON SALT
¼ CUP EVAPORATED CANE JUICE
1 TABLESPOON GROUND CINNAMON
¾ CUP PEELED AND CHOPPED APPLE
  (GALA RECOMMENDED)
¼ CUP CORN OR SAFFLOWER OIL
1¼ CUP WATER
1 TABLESPOON GLUTEN-FREE
  VANILLA EXTRACT

1. Preheat oven to 400°F.

2. Combine dry ingredients in a medium mixing bowl and stir until blended.

3. Add wet ingredients, including apple, and stir until the batter is smooth.

4. Pour batter into a glass or non-stick 8-inch baking dish (at least 1½ inches in height).

5. Bake 20 mins, or until cake is firm and golden brown. Cool slightly before serving.

Apple or Peach Crisp

FILLING

2 LARGE GALA APPLES OR PEACHES, PEELED AND SLICED

¼ CUP RAISINS

SWEETENER—½ CUP EVAPORATED CANE JUICE OR AGAVE NECTAR

1 TEASPOON GROUND CINNAMON

½ TEASPOON SALT

1 TABLESPOON CORN OR CANOLA OIL

1 TEASPOON GLUTEN-FREE VANILLA EXTRACT

CRUMB TOPPING

1 CUP QUINOA OR BUCKWHEAT FLOUR

½ CUP LIGHT BROWN SUGAR, LOOSELY PACKED

½ TEASPOON SALT

½ CUP PALM OIL SHORTENING

1 TEASPOON GROUND CINNAMON

1. Preheat oven to 350°F.

2. Combine filling ingredients in a bowl. Stir until blended. Pour into a 9-inch baking dish and set aside.

3. Prepare topping. Combine flour, brown sugar, cinnamon, shortening, and salt in a medium bowl. Sift with a fork until light and flaky. Use your fingers to sprinkle topping generously over apples.

4. Bake for 45-60 mins, until topping is light brown.

Fruit Sorbet (Raw)

3   CUPS OF ANY OF THE FOLLOWING
    FRUITS:
    STRAWBERRIES
    BLUEBERRIES
    PEELED AND PITTED MANGOS
    RASPBERRIES
½   CUP AGAVE NECTAR

1. Pour fruit and agave into a blender. Purée at high speed until the mixture becomes smooth.

2. Pour mixture into a glass bowl with a lid.

3. Cover and freeze. Serve frozen.

Gingerbread Cookies

1 CUP LIGHT BUCKWHEAT FLOUR
¼ TEASPOON SALT
¼ TEASPOON GROUND GINGER
    POWDER
¼ TEASPOON CINNAMON POWDER
¼ TEASPOON GROUND NUTMEG
¼ CUP LIGHT BROWN SUGAR, PACKED
¼ CUP EVAPORATED CANE JUICE
¼ CUP CORN OR SAFFLOWER OIL
1 TABLESPOON MOLASSES
¼ CUP WATER
VANILLA OR WHITE FROSTING FROM
    PAGE 210 FOR DECORATING

1. Preheat oven to 375°F.

2. In a small bowl, combine dry ingredients and stir to blend.

3. Add wet ingredients. Using an oiled spoon will keep the molasses from sticking.

4. Stir until a thick dough forms. Use hands to form a ball of dough.

   For flat, round cookies, use hands to make 1-inch balls of dough. Place on a cookie sheet and press down with fingers to flatten the cookie. Repeat, placing each ball three inches apart.

   For cookie cutter shapes, lightly dust a large, smooth surface (such as a cutting board) with light buckwheat flour. Place the dough on the surface and use hands or a rolling pin to flatten the dough into an 8 to 10-inch circle. Use cookie cutter to make as many shapes as possible. Scrape away excess dough with a butter knife. Use a metal spatula to place shapes on baking sheet. Gather excess dough and repeat.

5. Bake 15 mins, or until cookies are firm to the touch. Cool completely and decorate with Vanilla or White Frosting if desired.

Lemon-Cardamom Pound Cake

2 CUPS QUINOA FLOUR

2 TABLESPOONS LIGHT BUCKWHEAT
   FLOUR

2 TABLESPOONS TAPIOCA FLOUR

½ CUP EVAPORATED CANE JUICE

2 TABLESPOONS BAKING POWDER
   (ALUMINUM-FREE)

¼ TEASPOON SALT

1 TEASPOON GROUND CARDAMOM
   (OPTIONAL)

1 TEASPOON GROUND LEMON PEEL

½ CUP CORN OR SAFFLOWER OIL

1½ CUPS WATER

¼ CUP LEMON JUICE

LEMON GLAZE FROM PAGE 209

1. Preheat oven to 400°F.

2. In a medium mixing bowl, stir together dry ingredients. Add wet ingredients and stir until blended.

3. Pour batter into a glass or non-stick 9x5 loaf pan (at least 2 inches in height). Bake 25-30 mins.

4. Cool completely and spread Lemon Glaze over the top.

Strawberry Cake

2 CUPS LIGHT BUCKWHEAT FLOUR
2 TABLESPOONS TAPIOCA FLOUR
2 TABLESPOONS BAKING POWDER
   (ALUMINUM-FREE)
¼ TEASPOON SALT
½ CUP EVAPORATED CANE JUICE
½ CUP CORN OR SAFFLOWER OIL
2 CUPS WATER
1 CUP CHOPPED STRAWBERRIES
STRAWBERRY FROSTING RECIPE FROM
   PAGE 210

1. Preheat oven to 400°F.

2. In a medium bowl, combine dry ingredients and stir.

3. Add wet ingredients and stir until blended.

4. Add strawberries and stir very gently.

5. Pour into a 9-inch baking dish (at least 2 inches in height) or two 8-inch baking dishes (at least 1½ inches in height) and bake 20-25 mins. The center will be firm when done.

6. Cool completely and top with Strawberry Frosting.

Perfect Macaroons

1½ CUPS WATER
SWEETENER—1 CUP AGAVE NECTAR OR
   EVAPORATED CANE JUICE
2   TEASPOONS GLUTEN-FREE VANILLA
   EXTRACT
½   TEASPOON SALT
½   CUP LIGHT BUCKWHEAT FLOUR OR
   QUINOA FLOUR
3   CUPS FINELY SHREDDED COCONUT
   (UNSWEETENED)

1. Preheat oven to 375°F.

2. In a medium mixing bowl, combine water, sweetener, vanilla, and salt. Stir with a whisk until blended.

3. Add flour and coconut. Stir with a spoon until blended.

4. Drop batter by the tablespoon onto a non-stick baking sheet, 2 inches apart.

5. Bake for 15 mins or until macaroons appear light brown.

Sugar Cookies or Chocolate Chip Cookies

RECIPE 1

1   CUP LIGHT BUCKWHEAT FLOUR
½   TEASPOON BAKING SODA
¼   TEASPOON SALT
½   CUP LIGHT BROWN SUGAR, PACKED
¼   CUP PALM OIL SHORTENING
¼   CUP + 1 TABLESPOON WATER
1   TABLESPOON GLUTEN-FREE
    VANILLA EXTRACT
½   CUP GFCF CHOCOLATE CHIPS (FOR
    CHOCOLATE CHIP COOKIES)

1. Preheat oven to 400°F.

2. In a small mixing bowl, combine flour, baking soda, and salt. Stir to blend and set aside.

3. In a medium mixing bowl, combine brown sugar and shortening. Mix on low speed with an electric mixer until crumbly. Add water and vanilla, and continue to mix on low speed until the mixture has loosened.

4. Slowly add dry ingredients while mixing, until a smooth batter forms.

5. If using chocolate chips, gently stir them in with a spoon at this time.

6. Use a metal spoon to scoop 1 tablespoon of batter. Use a finger to slide the batter onto a cookie sheet (non-stick or parchment paper-lined). Continue by placing dough 3 inches apart, until all of the batter has been used.

7. Bake 20-25 mins. As they cool, the cookies will become crisp.

Note: be sure to use baking soda and not baking powder.

RECIPE 2

1   CUP QUINOA FLOUR
2   TEASPOONS TAPIOCA FLOUR
2   TEASPOONS POTATO FLOUR
2   TEASPOONS BAKING SODA
½   CUP LIGHT BROWN SUGAR
¼   CUP EVAPORATED CANE JUICE
2   TABLESPOONS PALM OIL
    SHORTENING
6   TABLESPOONS WATER
2   TABLESPOONS GLUTEN-FREE
    VANILLA EXTRACT
½   CUP GFCF CHOCOLATE CHIPS (FOR
    CHOCOLATE CHIP COOKIES)

1. Preheat oven to 350°F.

2. Combine dry ingredients in a medium bowl, including chocolate chips, if used.

3. Add wet ingredients and stir until a thick batter forms.

4. Use a metal spoon to scoop 1 tablespoon of batter. Use a finger to slide the batter onto a cookie sheet (non-stick or parchment paper-lined). Continue by placing dough 3 inches apart, until all of the batter has been used.

5. Bake 20-25 mins. As they cool, the cookies will become crisp.

Note: The two recipe options yield very similar results.
Recipe 1 has a slightly more "earthy flavor." Choose based on your preference and/or flour availability.

Sweet Potato Pie

CRUST

½ CUP LIGHT OR DARK BUCKWHEAT
   FLOUR
1 TABLESPOON TAPIOCA FLOUR
¼ TEASPOON SALT
1 TABLESPOON EVAPORATED CANE
   JUICE
1½ TEASPOONS BAKING POWDER
   (ALUMINUM-FREE)
2 TABLESPOONS CORN OR
   SAFFLOWER OIL
¼ CUP WATER (UP TO ¼ CUP MORE
   WATER IF USING DARK BUCKWHEAT
   FLOUR)
LIGHT OR DARK BUCKWHEAT FLOUR
   FOR DUSTING

FILLING

1½ CUPS COOKED SWEET POTATO
   (FRESH OR CANNED)
1 PINCH GROUND NUTMEG
1 TEASPOON GROUND CINNAMON
½ TEASPOON SALT
¼ CUP EVAPORATED CANE JUICE OR ¼
   CUP AGAVE NECTAR
1 TABLESPOON GLUTEN-FREE
   VANILLA EXTRACT (UP TO 1
   TABLESPOON MORE IF DESIRED)
2 TABLESPOONS WATER (UP TO 2
   TABLESPOONS MORE IF DESIRED
   FOR THINNER FILLING)

1. Preheat oven to 400°F.

2. Prepare crust. Stir together dry ingredients in a small bowl.

3. Add wet ingredients and stir. The dough will appear moist and fluffy. Use a rubber spatula to gather the dough into a mound in the bowl.

4. Use the spatula to guide the mound of dough onto the center of a 9-inch pie pan.

5. Dust the top of the dough lightly with buckwheat flour and use hands to press the dough evenly along the bottom and sides of the pie pan. Continue to dust lightly with flour if too sticky. Set aside.

6. Prepare filling. Combine all filling ingredients in a medium bowl. If using canned sweet potatoes that are already smooth, stir thoroughly with a spoon to blend. If using fresh sweet potatoes, or canned potatoes that are cut into chunks, use an electric hand mixer on medium speed to blend until smooth. Scrape the sides of the bowl often.

7. Pour the potato mixture over the crust and spread evenly. Bake 20-25 mins until the crust is firm and golden brown.

8. Cool completely.

   Note: this recipe yields a thin crust once the dough has been spread along the pie pan. For a thicker crust, double the crust recipe. Bake an additional 5-10 mins.

Warm Apple Drizzle

2 CUPS SLICED APPLES (PEELED OR UNPEELED)
1 TEASPOON GROUND CINNAMON
¼ TEASPOON SALT (OPTIONAL)
½ CUP RAW OR TOASTED PUMPKIN SEEDS, COARSELY CHOPPED IN A BLENDER
2 TABLESPOONS AGAVE NECTAR
2 TABLESPOONS FLAXSEED MEAL

1. Preheat oven to 400°F.

2. In a small mixing bowl, combine apple slices, cinnamon and salt. Stir with a spoon.

3. Place the apple mixture in an 8-inch baking dish.

4. Spread pumpkin seeds evenly over top of apples.

5. Drizzle agave nectar over apples.

6. Sprinkle flaxseed meal evenly over apples.

7. Bake uncovered for 15 mins or until apples are soft.

8. Serve warm.

Makes 2 servings

Vanilla Cake or Cupcakes

FLOUR OPTIONS:
1   CUP LIGHT BUCKWHEAT FLOUR
1   CUP QUINOA FLOUR
OR
2   CUPS LIGHT BUCKWHEAT FLOUR

2   TABLESPOONS TAPIOCA FLOUR
2   TABLESPOONS BAKING POWDER
    (ALUMINUM-FREE)
¼   TEASPOON SALT
½   CUP EVAPORATED CANE JUICE (UP
    TO ¼ CUP MORE IF DESIRED)
½   CUP CORN OR SAFFLOWER OIL
2   CUPS WATER
2   TABLESPOONS GLUTEN-FREE
    VANILLA EXTRACT
DESIRED FLAVORED FROSTING FROM
    PAGE 210.

1. Preheat oven to 400°F.

2. In a medium bowl, combine dry ingredients and stir.

3. Add wet ingredients and stir until blended.

4. Pour into a 9-inch baking dish (at least 2 inches in height), two 8-inch baking dishes (at least 1.5 inches in height) or a lined muffin pan.

5. Bake 35-40 mins if using cake pan and 30-35 mins if using muffin pan. The center will be firm when done.

6. Cool completely and top with Flavored Frosting.

Note: The quinoa and buckwheat flour combination is highly recommended for lighter color and taste.

Velvet Pudding (Raw)

2 LARGE AVOCADOS, PEELED AND
  PITTED
¼ CUP UNSWEETENED COCOA
½ CUP RAW SUGAR OR AGAVE NECTAR

1. Mix all ingredients on low speed with an electric mixer until well blended. Scrape sides of the bowl often with a rubber spatula.

2. If using raw sugar, continue to blend until the sugar is dissolved.

3. Chill and serve.

> "Autists are the ultimate square peg, and the problem with pounding a square peg into a round hole is not that the hammering is hard work. It is that you're destroying the peg."
> —Paul Collins, Author

Fun Snacks

Chili Boats

5 SMALL RED POTATOES (TO MAKE
  2-INCH CIRCULAR SLICES)
½ TEASPOON SALT
1 TABLESPOON OLIVE OIL
2 CUPS CHILI (RECIPE FROM PAGE 12)
CHOPPED CILANTRO AND SCALLIONS.

1. Preheat oven to 400°F.

2. Wash and pat dry the potatoes. Slice the potatoes to make circles.

3. Place the potatoes in a medium mixing bowl, add oil and salt, and stir until blended.

4. Place the potato slices onto a non-stick baking sheet.

5. Bake for 30-40 mins until potatoes are soft. Let cool completely. Scoop a teaspoon of warm chili and place on top of each potato. Garnish with chopped cilantro and sliced scallions, if desired.

Sesame Submarine (Raw)

3 100% CORN CAKES
½ CUP SESAME BUTTER (FROM RECIPE
   ON PAGE 203)
FRESH BLUEBERRIES
FRESH STRAWBERRIES, CHOPPED

1. Cut corn cakes into fourths to make wedges.

2. Drop 1 tablespoon of sesame butter on the middle of each wedge. Top with fresh fruit.

Essential Fondue
(Fun, Nutritious, Raw)

1 CUP RAW CACAO POWDER
1 CUP RAW AGAVE NECTAR
1 TABLESPOON RAW COCONUT OIL
¼ TEASPOON SEA SALT (OPTIONAL)
FRESH FRUIT OF YOUR CHOICE FOR
    DIPPING

1. Combine cacao powder, agave, oil, and salt in a small bowl.

1. Mix thoroughly until smooth. Use as a dip for fresh fruit. Enjoy!

Trail Mix (Raw)

½ CUP FRESH COCONUT, DRIED AND
  SHREDDED
½ CUP DRIED CRANBERRIES
½ CUP RAISINS
1 CUP RAW PUMPKIN SEEDS
1 CUP RAW SUNFLOWER SEEDS
1 TABLESPOON OIL
1 TEASPOON SALT

1. Combine all ingredients in a bowl.

2. Toss until blended.

3. Enjoy!

For a non-raw alternative, heat ingredients in a non-stick pan over low heat. Toss constantly until lightly toasted.

"This Mother's Day, do me a personal favor. Find a Mom with a child that has special needs and give them a hug. Better yet, offer to watch the child so she can get a cup of coffee, take a long walk with a friend or simply sit and read uninterrupted for an hour.
—Rickey and Lisa Scarbrough, Maggieshope.org

Toppings, Glazes, and Sauces

Balsamic Fusion (Raw)

3   SMALL GARLIC CLOVES, MINCED
3   FRESH BASIL LEAVES, CHOPPED
¼   CUP RAW AGAVE NECTAR
½   TEASPOON SEA SALT
½   TEASPOON GROUND BLACK PEPPER
½   CUP BALSAMIC VINEGAR
JUICE OF 1 LARGE LEMON
UP TO ½ CUP COLD-PRESSED OLIVE OIL

1. Combine garlic, basil, agave, salt, black pepper, vinegar, and lemon juice in a small bowl. Stir with a whisk until blended.

2. Continue to stir while slowly adding olive oil. Taste frequently to test. Salad dressing should be equally sweet and sour.

Serving suggestion: Toss into salad. Use romaine lettuce, cucumbers, green peppers, dried cranberries, Mandarin oranges, and uncured bacon bits.

Barbecue Sauce

2 CUPS TOMATO SAUCE

1 CUP LIGHT BROWN SUGAR, PACKED

3 TABLESPOONS RAW, UNFILTERED APPLE CIDER VINEGAR

2 TABLESPOONS EXTRA-VIRGIN OLIVE OIL

2 TABLESPOONS MUSTARD POWDER

1 TABLESPOON ONION POWDER

1 TEASPOON SALT

1. Combine all ingredients in a small bowl. Stir well with a whisk until sugar is dissolved.

2. Spread over baked or grilled chicken or use for Sloppy Joe recipe on page 42.

3. Refrigerate leftovers until ready to use.

Fried Onion Topping

1   DICED ONION
¼   CUP CORNMEAL
½   TEASPOON SALT (OPTIONAL)
OIL FOR DEEP FRYING

1. Heat oil in a deep fryer.

2. In a medium mixing bowl, combine diced onion, cornmeal, and salt. Toss until onion is covered in cornmeal.

3. Using a slotted spatula, scoop up some of the mixture, allowing excess cornmeal to drop back into the bowl.

4. Place in hot oil and fry until light brown.

5. Cool completely. Crumble with your fingertips and serve over mashed potatoes.

Chicken or Beef Gravy

1 CUP CHICKEN OR BEEF BROTH (ROOM TEMPERATURE)
¼ CUP POTATO FLOUR OR LIGHT BUCKWHEAT FLOUR
2 TABLESPOONS CORN OR SAFFLOWER OIL
2 TABLESPOONS ONION, CHOPPED
SALT AND BLACK PEPPER TO TASTE

1. Combine broth and flour in a small bowl.

2. Stir with a whisk until flour is dissolved. Set aside.

3. Use a small saucepan to heat oil over medium heat.

4. Add onions and sauté until slightly brown. Reduce heat to low.

5. Slowly pour broth/flour mixture into the saucepan. Stir constantly with a whisk.

6. Gravy will thicken. Remove from heat when desired thickness has been achieved.

7. Add salt and pepper to taste.

Serve warm over Cornbread Stuffing on page 68 or Fluffy Mashed potatoes on page 70.

Sesame or Pumpkin Seed "Butter" (Raw)

1½ CUPS RAW SESAME SEEDS OR
  PUMPKIN SEEDS
UP TO ½ CUP UNREFINED SAFFLOWER
  OIL
2 TEASPOONS SEA SALT
½ CUP RAW AGAVE NECTAR

1. Combine seeds, ¼ cup oil, and salt in a blender.

2. Purée at a high speed for several mins, adding oil by the tablespoon during blending to reach desired thickness.

3. Add sweetener and mix briefly until blended.

   Use as a dip for grilled chicken or warm corn tortillas.
   For a non-raw alternative, use lightly roasted seeds. This will enhance the flavor of the seed "butter."

Cider-Flax Salad Dressing (Raw)

1   CUP RAW APPLE CIDER VINEGAR
½   CUP COLD-PRESSED FLAXSEED OIL
    (UNFILTERED)
½   CUP RAW AGAVE NECTAR
½   TEASPOON SEA SALT

1. Combine all ingredients and blend with a whisk.

2. Toss into salad with lettuce, raisins, cucumbers, and shredded carrots.

Citrus-Ginger Salad Dressing (Raw)

JUICE OF 1 LARGE ORANGE

¼ CUP RAW APPLE CIDER VINEGAR

3 TABLESPOONS COLD-PRESSED OLIVE OIL

1 TEASPOON FRESH GINGER, PEELED AND MINCED

1 TEASPOON SEA SALT

2 TABLESPOONS RAW AGAVE NECTAR

1 TEASPOON RAW SESAME SEEDS

1. Combine all ingredients in a small mixing bowl.

2. Whisk until all ingredients are well blended.

3. Toss into salad with sliced cucumbers, thinly sliced carrots, and dried cranberries.

Optional: For enhanced flavor, stir in 2 tablespoons of fresh coconut water.

Flavored Glazes

CHOCOLATE GLAZE
1   CUP POWDERED SUGAR
2   TABLESPOONS COCOA POWDER
3   TABLESPOONS WATER

MILD LEMON OR ORANGE GLAZE
1   CUP POWDERED SUGAR
1   TABLESPOON LEMON OR ORANGE
    JUICE (FRESH OR BOTTLED)
2   TABLESPOONS WATER
OPTIONAL: 1 TEASPOON FINELY
    CHOPPED LEMON OR ORANGE PEEL

STRAWBERRY GLAZE
1   CUP POWDERED SUGAR
1   TABLESPOON VERY RIPE, MASHED
    STRAWBERRY
1   TEASPOON WATER

TANGY LEMON OR ORANGE GLAZE
1   CUP POWDERED SUGAR
3   TABLESPOONS LEMON JUICE OR
    ORANGE JUICE (USE FRESHLY-
    SQUEEZED FRUIT FOR BEST FLAVOR)
OPTIONAL: 1 TEASPOON FINELY
    CHOPPED LEMON OR ORANGE PEEL

VANILLA GLAZE
1   CUP POWDERED SUGAR
1   TABLESPOON VANILLA EXTRACT
2   TABLESPOONS WATER

WHITE GLAZE
1   CUP POWDERED SUGAR
3   TABLESPOONS WATER.

1. Combine ingredients in a small bowl.

2. Stir until a smooth glaze forms.

3. Spread over baked goods. The glaze will harden slightly within 30 mins.

Flavored Frostings

CHOCOLATE FROSTING

2   CUPS POWDERED SUGAR
2   TABLESPOONS PALM OIL
    SHORTENING
½   CUP COCOA POWDER
3   TABLESPOONS WATER (UP TO ¼
    TABLESPOON MORE FOR THINNER
    FROSTING)

STRAWBERRY OR BLUEBERRY
FROSTING

2   CUPS POWDERED SUGAR
2   TABLESPOONS PALM OIL
    SHORTENING
2   TABLESPOONS FRESH, RIPE
    STRAWBERRIES OR BLUEBERRIES,
    FULLY MASHED WITH A FORK
    (MEASURE AFTER MASHED)

VANILLA FROSTING

2   CUPS POWDERED SUGAR
2   TABLESPOONS PALM OIL
    SHORTENING
2   TABLESPOONS GLUTEN-FREE
    VANILLA EXTRACT
1   TABLESPOON WATER

WHITE FROSTING

2 CUPS POWDERED SUGAR
2 TABLESPOONS PALM OIL SHORTENING
2 TABLESPOONS WATER

1. Combine all ingredients in a bowl.

2. Stir until a smooth frosting forms. If using fruit, thickness will depend on ripeness of fruit. Add water by the teaspoon if desired for thinner frosting.

3. Use with favorite baked goods.

Honey Mustard Dipping Sauce

½ CUP HONEY

2 TEASPOONS MUSTARD POWDER

¼ CUP RAW, UNFILTERED APPLE CIDER VINEGAR

¼ TEASPOON SALT (OPTIONAL)

1. Combine all ingredients in a small bowl.

2. Stir with a spoon until well blended.

3. Use as a dip for chicken nuggets, chicken strips, sliced fruit, or vegetable sticks.

French Salad Dressing and Marinade

½ CUP TOMATO SAUCE (USE TOMATO PASTE FOR A THICKER DRESSING)
½ CUP APPLE CIDER VINEGAR
¼ CUP MOLASSES
1 TEASPOON EACH OF SALT AND ONION POWDER
¼ CUP EXTRA VIRGIN OLIVE OIL

1. Combine all ingredients in a mixing bowl. Whisk until well blended.

2. Cover and keep chilled until ready to use.

3. Use as a meat marinade or serve over salad.

French Salad Dressing and Marinade (Raw)

2 LARGE TOMATOES
½ CUP ONION, CHOPPED
½ CUP RAW APPLE CIDER VINEGAR
¼ CUP RAW AGAVE NECTAR
¼ CUP COLD PRESSED OLIVE OIL
1 TEASPOON SEA SALT

1. Combine all ingredients in a blender and blend at high speed until smooth.

2. Chill until ready to use.

3. Toss into salad with shredded carrots and raisins. It can also be used as a marinade for grilling meats.

Healing Arts for Children with Autism

Human bodies have seven "chakras" that are the main energy centers of the body. They are located from the top of the head to the bottom of the torso. "Healing Arts," as named in Western society, are therapies that help balance the flow of energy in each chakra. Our cells have a constant flow of energy, which results in what we know as human life. Environmental and physical stressors can cause the energy to flow either too fast or too slow. The slower the energy moves, the more susceptible we become to illnesses and stress. An even, steady flow of energy results in increased health and feeling happy and energized.

Everyone can benefit from Healing Arts, especially children with autism. Balanced energy flow (or balanced chakras) results in optimal functioning throughout the whole body, which compliments the use of traditional therapies such as diet, speech, physical therapy, or ABA (Applied Behavior Analysis).

Most people cannot see the chakras with the human eye, but the effects of balanced or off-balanced chakras can be felt. Each chakra has a corresponding physical system:

The root chakra (located at the base of the torso) corresponds with the large intestine, rectum, kidneys, and adrenal glands.

The navel chakra (located at the navel) corresponds to the reproduction system, testicles, ovaries, bladder, and kidneys.
The solar plexus chakra (located at the diaphragm) corresponds to the liver, gall bladder, stomach, spleen, small intestine, and pancreas.
The heart chakra (located at the heart) corresponds to the heart, arms, and thymus gland.
The throat chakra (located at the throat) corresponds to the lungs, throat, and thyroid gland.
The third eye chakra (located at the forehead, between the eyebrows) corresponds to the brain, face, and pituitary gland.
The crown chakra (located on the crown of the head) corresponds to the whole being and the pineal gland.

There are many Healing Art techniques (or chakra balancing techniques) including Reiki, yoga, tai chi, meditation, color therapy, visualization, and aromatherapy. In this book, I will discuss Reiki, yoga, and meditation—three essential parts of our son's treatment plan.

REIKI

Reiki is a Japanese method for promoting healing through the laying of hands. This results in the arousing of the body's own healing response. It is a non-invasive, drug-free technique that balances the flow of energy through the body and brings harmony to the whole person. For individuals who are sensitive to touch, Reiki can be done without touching. Reiki is commonly used to enhance traditional medical therapies.

During a Reiki treatment, patients feel a warm sense of relaxation and lightness. Such deep relaxation has a positive impact on physical health, emotional health, relationships, will power, motivation, self-esteem, and more. While many people experience a cumulative effect of Reiki over several treatments, some people do report instant, life-changing experiences.

How Can Reiki Help Children with Autism?

Often, children with autism experience anxiety in social interactions and new situations. Children can also be highly susceptible to the stress and anxiety of their caregivers. Anxiety can result in problems with sleep, digestion, focus, and attention. In my experience as a practitioner, Reiki has helped children with autism to relax, sleep better, and feel more secure. While most Reiki sessions are performed while the patient is laying down, it is perfectly okay for a child to continue moving and playing while receiving a Reiki treatment. The energy will flow regardless of what the individual is doing. My son has become accustomed to laying down (and often falling asleep) during Reiki. However, I have found that allowing active children to explore works just as well. After a while, even their interactive play becomes more relaxed.

Many children on the autism spectrum face problems with "sensory integration." Sensory challenges can include over- or under-sensitivity to touch, sight, hearing, and taste. Reiki and other healing arts help us gain an awareness of our bodies in relation to space. The more comfortable we feel in the space around us, the more organized our senses flow, thus, the better equipped we are to handle change and variety in sight, hearing, taste, and touch.

YOGA

Yoga is an ancient healing art originating in India. It integrates exercise, breathing, and meditation to help the person gain balance in all areas of life. Hatha yoga is one of six branches of yoga most commonly used in the West, focusing on poses.

Yoga offers countless benefits for everyone. When a series of poses are combined into a routine, the person gains increased body awareness, physical flexibility, and muscle tone. The breathing that is integrated into the routine results in relaxation and centeredness.

How Can Yoga Help Children with Autism?

Children on the autism spectrum can benefit greatly from yoga:

- Breath work results in deep relaxation, anxiety relief, focus, and some have reported reduced blood pressure and hyperactivity.
- Inverted poses provide deep pressure, which stimulates the vestibular system.
- Upward poses provide energy, alertness, and increased mood.
- All poses result in increased muscle tone, balance, and flexibility.

MEDITATION

Meditation is an awareness of inner silence. The Latin root of the word, meditation (*mederi*), means "to heal." The purpose of meditating is to achieve mental, emotional, and physical balance, which promotes healing on all levels. Meditation is beneficial for everyone, especially for parents of autistic children, helping them to find reserves of patience and energy at challenging times. More and more medical professionals are recommending meditation as an intervention for high blood pressure, heart ailments, asthma, anxiety, and insomnia.

While it does not require any specific training or teaching, meditation becomes easier with practice. When my family and I started using meditation, we found it difficult to sit quietly for even fifteen seconds. We were constantly distracted by the stimulation of the world around us and the never ending to-do list. However, the more we practiced, the longer we were able to sit still, adding two to three mins each week.

How Can Parents and Their Children with Autism Use Meditation?

Awareness of inner silence gives us respite from constant negative "chatter" in our subconscious minds. Stressful social encounters, physical pain, television images, and fear can feed into the "negative talk." During meditation, take the time to first become silent and as still as possible. This can be accomplished by counting ten slow breaths or by focusing on a beautiful object, such as a shiny marble. Once silent, focus your thoughts on a phrase such as, "I am healthy and safe." You can say it out loud or silently for as long as you can. If you are meditating with a child, encourage him or her to imagine something he or she loves, such as a puppy or a favorite toy. Remember that it is okay if you only get through ten seconds at a time or if your child is nonverbal and cannot repeat phrases. This is simply a guide. Keep practicing whatever "quieting" activity your child can accomplish. You will find that it will become easier and will last longer as time goes on.

Autism Resource Listing

Natural Treatment Centers, Practitioners and Information

Dr. Peter Bauth, D.C. LCP (404) 317-7715

Brain Balance Achievement Centers (www.brainbalancecenters.com)

Mary Riposo, PhD (www.integratedenergyhealing.com) (email: mary@integratedenergyhealing.com)

The Center for Integrated Manual Therapy (Center IMT) (www.centerimt.com)

Dr. Daemon Jones, Healthy Daes Naturopathic Center (www.healthydaes.org)

Autism Research Institute (www.autism.com)

Defeat Autism Now (DAN) conferences

National Institutes of Health, National Center for Complementary and Alternative Medicine (www.nccam.nih.gov)

Support Groups and Advocacy

Talk About Curing Autism (www.tacanow.org)

Autism Society (www.autism-society.org)

Autism Speaks (www.autismspeaks.org)

National Vaccine Information Center (www.nvic.org)

Maggie's Hope (www.maggieshope.org)

Supplementation

Kirkman Labs (www.kirkmanlabs.com)

Nutri-West (www.nutriwest.com)

Bluebonnet (www.bluebonnetnutrition.com)

Nordic Naturals (www.nordicnaturals.com

Barlean's (www.barleans.com)

GFCF Grocery (See also "Using This Book" section on page xv)

Bouchard Family Farms (light buckwheat flour) (www.ployes.com)

The Birkett Mills (www.thebirkettmills.com)

Enjoy Life (www.enjoylifefoods.com)

Arrowhead Mills (www.arrowheadmills.com)

Bob's Red Mill (www.bobsredmill.com)

Kinnikinnick Foods (consumer.kinnikinnick.com)

Ancient Harvest Quinoa (www.quinoa.net)

Wellshire Farms (www.Wellshirefarms.com)

Tools for Families and Children

Lamit Bear & the Feel Better Pals (www.lamitbear.com)

Chynna Laird, Author (www.chynna-laird-author.com)

Adonya Wong, Author (www.adonyawong.com)

Yoga Kids DVDs (www.gaiam.com)

Since We're Friends book by Celeste Shally

It's Hip Hop Baby! DVD's for speech and language (www.itshiphopbaby.com)

Baby Bumble Bee (www.babybumblebee.com)

Glossary and Information

AGAVE NECTAR: Nectar derived from a cactus-like agave plant, used for sweetening. Its consistency and color are similar to that of honey.

AUTISM: A neurological disorder that affects development, communication, and social functioning. Many children with Autism have progressed considerably by eliminating gluten (from wheat, rye, and barley) and casein (from cow's milk) from their diets.

BUCKWHEAT: Buckwheat is a gluten-free plant closely related to rhubarb. Buckwheat is not related to wheat, and it is not a grain. However, buckwheat holds nutritional value that exceeds many whole grains. The seed can be finely ground to produce flour for baking or can be cooked and consumed as a side dish.

CASEIN: A protein found in cow's milk that closely resembles gluten. It provides elasticity and makes foods such as cheese, yogurt, and cow's milk "gooey."

CELIAC DISEASE: This is an autoimmune disease resulting in damage to the small intestine when gluten (from wheat, barley, or rye) is consumed. Many people who have this disease choose a gluten-free, casein-free diet (GFCF). It is also best to completely avoid oat. Celiac disease is not the same as wheat allergy.

CROSS-CONTAMINATION: The passing of an allergen indirectly from one source to another through improperly cleaned hands, equipment, procedures, or products.

ELIMINATION DIET: see page ix.

EMR POISONING (ELECTROMAGNETIC RADIATION): This is harmful radiation that emanates from almost all technology, electrical gadgets, and radio waves. Over-exposure to radiation has been proven to cause brain tumors, hyperactivity, disease, and contamination of food, air, and water supply.

EVAPORATED CANE JUICE: A granule sweetener made from sugar cane that is less processed than traditional white, refined sugar, and therefore more nutritious. This product does not spike blood sugar as quickly as white, refined sugar does.

FEINGOLD DIET: see page viii.

FLAXSEED: This is the seed of a flax plant that has multiple health benefits, including lowering cholesterol, boosting immunity, fighting constipation, and combating heart disease. It is a source of soluble and insoluble dietary fiber. The flax plant's fibers are used for clothing. Its seeds are used for food.

FOOD ALLERGY: This is an adverse reaction to a food involving the immune system. The body identifies the food as harmful and creates antibodies called IgE to fight it off. Eventually, histamines rush into the bloodstream, causing eczema, hives, sinus and throat swelling, breathing difficulty, diarrhea, a drop in blood pressure, and many other symptoms.

FOOD INTOLERANCE/ FOOD SENSITIVITY: This is an adverse reaction to a food involving the digestive system. The body has difficulty in producing sufficient amounts of digestive enzymes to break down the food. Some signs and symptoms may resemble an allergic reaction (diarrhea, vomiting, heartburn, and many other symptoms).

GLUTEN: A protein found in wheat, barley, rye, and spelt. It provides elasticity in breads, crusts, and pastries and makes foods "gooey." Oat does not contain gluten, but its protein has a very similar make up as gluten. Also, oat has a high chance for gluten contamination during its harvesting on wheat fields. Many people who wish to completely avoid gluten do not use oat products.

HEALING ARTS: A western term used to describe therapeutic activities that balance chakras, or energy flow in the body (yoga, martial arts, tai chi, meditation, Reiki). Healing Arts are used to complement traditional medical care.

HISTAMINE: A chemical released by the body during an allergic reaction. Histamines are what trigger physical symptoms such as eczema, hives, sinus and throat swelling, diarrhea, drop in blood pressure, and many others.

HYPOALLERGENIC: This describes a food or substance that contains low or no amounts of common allergens, minimizing a person's chance for an allergic reaction. For example, some cosmetic or household products may omit perfumes or dyes. Some food products may omit nuts, milk, or other common allergens to lower the risk for an allergic reaction by the consumer.

IMMUNOGLOBULIN E (IgE): A type of antibody released by the immune system, primarily to protect the body from allergens. IgE signals the release of histamines that trigger physical symptoms of an allergic reaction.

IMMUNOGLOBULIN G (IgG): A type of antibody released from the body when a food sensitivity culprit is consumed, triggering adverse digestive symptoms.

IONIC FOOT BATH: A warm water bath with a positively-charged magnet, used to "pull" toxins (which have a negative charge) from the body through the open pores of the feet.

MEDITATION: A soothing Healing Art that balances energy through quiet reflection, affirmation, breathing, and visualization.

ORGANIC: Organic crops have been grown without the use of chemicals or Genetically Modified Organisms (GMOs). Organic meats do not contain antibiotics or growth hormones. Organic foods are primarily chemical-free and processed less. Therefore, they are much easier to digest and have a higher nutritional value. See (xi) "Going Organic" for details about organic foods.

QUINOA SEED: Quinoa is an ancient leafy plant that holds extraordinary nutritional value (including protein, essential amino acids, fiber, iron, and magnesium). Like buckwheat, quinoa seeds are used to produce flour or they can be cooked in a variety of ways and eaten as a side dish.

RAW: Food is considered to be raw if it is not heated above 118°F. Fruits, vegetables, and seeds are used in this book in raw recipes. Other items used in raw recipes (not used in this book) include nuts and sprouted grains. A common method for preparing raw recipes is dehydrating. Dehydrating helps produce various textures without officially cooking the food. Cooking a food above 118°F destroys the majority of the digestive enzymes and nutrients. Including as much raw foods as possible in the diet helps improve the digestive process that gives a boost to the immune system.

REIKI: This is a non-invasive Healing Art that balances energy flow in the body through laying of hands.

SALICYLATES: A chemical that is either added to foods or naturally occurring in foods. It is a common culprit for sensitivity and is one of the items excluded in the Feingold Diet approach.

SPECIFIC CARBOHYDRATE DIET: see page ix.

TOXINS: Toxins are poisonous substances that have adverse effects on health. They exist in everyday living—in the commercial food supply, air, water, medicines, and even in the form of electromagnetic fields. In a healthy person, the immune system will combat poisonous substances, and the digestive and excretory systems will expel them from the body.

YOGA: A healing art that balances the flow of energy in the body through movement and breathwork.

Index

Notes:

My Favorite Recipes:

The Autism Cookbook